C000139575

The Off-Modern

Psychology Estranged

The Off-Modern

Psychology Estranged

Ron Roberts

Winchester, UK
Washington, USA

First published by Zero Books, 2017
Zero Books is an imprint of John Hunt Publishing Ltd., Laurel House, Station Approach,
Alresford, Hants, SO24 9JH, UK
office1@jhpbooks.net
www.johnhuntpublishing.com
www.zero-books.net

For distributor details and how to order please visit the 'Ordering' section on our website.

Text copyright: Ron Roberts 2016

ISBN: 978 1 78535 595 0
978 1 78535 596 7 (Hardcover)
Library of Congress Control Number: 2016951898

All rights reserved. Except for brief quotations in critical articles or reviews, no part of this
book may be reproduced in any manner without prior written permission from the publishers.

The rights of Ron Roberts as author have been asserted in accordance with the Copyright,
Designs and Patents Act 1988.

A CIP catalogue record for this book is available from the British Library.

Design: Stuart Davies

Printed and bound by CPI Group (UK) Ltd, Croydon, CR0 4YY, UK

We operate a distinctive and ethical publishing philosophy in all
areas of our business, from our global network of authors to
production and worldwide distribution.

CONTENTS

And I – at odds with the obedient world rejoice
– Osip Mandelstam

Science is powerless to solve the enigma of being
– Lee Smolin

The voyage of discovery lies not in finding new landscapes, but in having new eyes
– Marcel Proust

In memory of Svetlana
And to Musa and Yury Goldberg

Preface

"Trace the lineage of any significant event," wrote Rebecca Solnit (2013, p.69), "and coincidences and strangers appear from beyond the horizon of the calculable." This book owes everything to the improbable and incalculable horizon brought near. An unlikely though fortuitous chain of events can be traced back at least to the late 1990s when I began to research the relationship between debt and health in students. Following the ending of mandatory grants and the introduction of tuition fees I saw the systemic introduction of debt into the pecuniary life of the student population as an opportunity to apply the methodology I had learned, during a prior spell in epidemiology, so as to document and track the effects of financial adversity on young people's health and well-being. One strand of this work concerned passage through the labyrinth of higher education being enabled through participation in the sex industry. This was a topic which garnered the attention of the press – both salubrious and serious. On one such occasion a Russian journalist based in London contacted me to discuss the prospects of running a story on the topic. When we met, she was hoping I'd be able to put her in touch with one or two student sex workers to interview face to face. I explained that because of the ethical constraints of confidentiality and anonymity necessarily afforded to all research participants this wouldn't be possible. Disappointed, she wanted to know what other research I'd been engaged in that might also grab her interest. At the time I had not long finished a piece of work for colleagues in Bosnia who had asked me to write a critical piece on life in the Western world. Following the break-up of the former Yugoslavia and the horrors of the Bosnian war, many in Bosnia have set their sights on a future refuge from insecurity in membership of the Western institutions of NATO and the European Union. The Bosnians wished

1

to compare my critical vision with their imagined oasis of economic and political safety. I gave the piece I'd written to the journalist. A phrase I'd used in the article proved to be more than lucky. In discussing the end of Western dreams of an ever-brighter and improving world, I remarked that we had now entered a state of affairs in which we had become "nostalgic for the future." This phrase caught my journalist acquaintance's eye. She immediately asked me if I had read a book by Svetlana Boym entitled *The Future of Nostalgia*. Though I had not, her enthusiastic endorsement convinced me to look it up.

My copy of Svetlana's book duly arrived and in the course of the following month or two I set about reading it. I was bowled over by this extraordinary work and took, for me, the unusual step of writing to her (this was in early June 2014) to tell her how much I'd enjoyed her book. Described in cyberspace as "a text for wandering spirits," it is a rich essay on longing and belonging pursued through the twists and turns of European history, philosophy, aesthetics, politics and art. It defies conventional academic boundaries and most unusually mixes personal narrative and incisive analysis with unrivalled poetic flair. Beautifully written, thought-provoking and moving, I told her that I considered it to be not only the best work on social and collective memory (another one of my research interests) but also full of the humanity I felt my own discipline (psychology) lacked. I was genuinely sorry that my pleasure in reading it had come to an end. Svetlana graciously replied within a week and indicated her own curiosity about my views on the lack of humanity in psychology. I duly responded and in turn we exchanged several warm letters exploring a range of ideas and detailing, on both sides, what Svetlana described as "snippets of experience." In due course Svetlana mentioned that she would be passing through London, en route from Vienna where she was making a film. This opened up the prospect of continuing our interdisciplinary transatlantic conversations in person – an opportunity which we both took. On July 22nd I headed back to London from an Open University summer school in Brighton – I'd fortunately been given the afternoon off – and we met. It was outside Westminster station on the bridge underneath Thomas Thorneycroft's imposing statue of Boadicea, riding into battle on her two-horse chariot. The next few hours passed by as an extended treat in the intangible present, a treat which was extended still further a few days later as Svetlana was able to change her scheduled flight back to the US and stay in the capital a while longer. On a typical English summer day, alternating between torrential rain and blazing sun, we had a boat ride to Greenwich followed by a lazy and timeless adventure on London's South Bank, where we cemented a newfound friendship. Over the following year we occasionally Skyped, swapped innumerable text messages and emails and decided we would be friends for life.

In Eduardo Galeano's *Book of Embraces* there is a brief allegorical tale. In this we are told the world "is a heap of people, a sea of tiny flames" and each of these "shines with his or her own light. No two flames are alike. There are big flames and little flames, flames of every colour. Some people's flames are so still they don't even flicker in the wind, while others have wild flames that fill the air with sparks. Some foolish flames neither burn nor shed light, but others blaze with life so fiercely that you can't look at them without blinking and if you approach, you shine in fire." Svetlana's flame blazed fiercely, with an elegance and assuredness firmly rooted to the earth. It was difficult not to feel one's own mind on fire in conversation with her and not to have loved her would have been like trying to defy gravity.

From one of our chats – begun in Greenwich Park over a cup of tea and a cake, and continued beneath the bright night lights on the South Bank a few hours later – emerged the idea that I could perhaps pursue my desire for a discipline of the human condition by exploring her concept of the "off-modern" in relation to the possibilities it offers for psychology. This book is the result, my own (off) take on the human mystery and a suggestion of another way to do psychology and know thyself. Early in our correspondence Svetlana asked me whether I thought psychology's malaise was because there was no longer time and space within it to tell nuanced individual stories. I firmly believe that psychology must always have a place for storytelling so I have endeavoured to include a few in these pages, beginning with this tale of the genesis of the book. In all my letters to Svetlana I invariably signed off with the same three words: "until next time." For me Svetlana's work pointed to the stars – both literally[1] and metaphorically. Sadly, with her untimely passing, she will no longer reach them, nor will they bend down to lend assistance. There will be no more next times, and the world for all its joys will remain a poorer and less colourful place without her. Galeano's simple tale is instructive. In the midst of the unseemly chaos and inhumanity that surrounds us we must not forget that we can make a difference – that fire is contagious and that we can help light the way for one another.

Acknowledgements

As always I must thank my lifelong friend Merry Cross who has helped me with reading, discussing and editing what follows. Her acquaintance, like all friendship, is a great gift and in Merry's case an extraordinary one. Additional thanks to all my other friends, to Subi and Wandia and to Kevin Howells who many years ago gave me an opening in academic life. Thanks also to everyone at Zero Books.

One

Introduction: Psychology, Old and New?

I always thought psychology goes on in the writing. So one of the questions I used to ask was how do you write psychology? Well, you must write it so that it touches the soul, or it's not psychology. It has to have that moving quality of experience, and that means it has to have many sorts of metaphors and absurdities and things that go with life. Otherwise you're writing an academic or a scientific description of something but it's no longer psychology
– James Hillman (in Hillman & Shamdasani, 2013, p.200)

The truly important thing is to discover the conditions of life
– Walter Benjamin (1999, p.147)

The art and practice of attempting to make sense of the human condition, to follow the flow of what Baudelaire (2010, p.33) described as "the great rivers of the human heart," has almost entirely disappeared from contemporary psychology. It has joined the long list of activities superseded by the relentless onward march of scientific rationalism with its accompanying misplaced belief that wisdom comes through technological prowess (Burak, 2016). Any attempt to grasp the essence of the human organism, to be deemed worthy, must be evidently "modern" and measurable – willing and able to keep at arm's length what the artist Paul Cezanne referred to as the "rainbow of chaos." The "strange, the disorderly and the uncertain" (Starosta, 2007, p.147), what Freud referred to as the "uncanny," much of the rich complexity and quirkiness that makes human life interesting, has been pushed aside: it is a quest for intellectual respectability and, it must be said, a media-driven aesthetic to convey the essential and by now expected technological gee-whizz factor in the fifteen seconds or so available before the presumed attention span of the audience disappears down a black hole. This is not a recipe for deep thinking. The irony is that in this modernist quest to advance psychological science, it is the very trappings of modernity, "the transient, the fleeting, the contingent" (Baudelaire, 2010, p.17) present in human life, which are most easily overlooked in the search for enduring universals. Baudelaire set his critical gaze on the relationship between industry and art – seeing the former as the "mortal enemy" (ibid, p.110) of the latter.

The sceptical gaze of the modern (public) critic however is seldom directed to the problematic relation between industry and science. While art critics exist in abundance and regularly dispense their wares to the viewing and reading public, media critics of science are to be noted for their absence, with the long cold reach of Big Science and Big Pharma being acknowledged concerns only for political activists, disgruntled beneficiaries of dysfunctional psychiatry and that rare breed of critical psychologists and psychotherapists. A public appetite for critical science is one to which editors and proprietors remain oblivious. Social science meanwhile remains a distant speck on the televisual horizon. But what is presumed newsworthy about art rarely extends beyond the cost a work may fetch at auction or whether the performance and display of it is deemed worthy of public attention in the form of bums on theatre seats or a physical presence in galleries. The effect that a given work may have on one's outlook or understanding of the world is often no more than an afterthought. Art is commercial in a different sense to science. Science by comparison is reckoned to be of import only by virtue of its capacity to generate (or be a party to) industrial innovation; novel copy regarding dubious medical break-throughs (cures for cancer treated as a single-disease entity top the list); the latest technological developments in the digital sphere; unreplicated findings about the human brain; and the occasional glimpse of outer space. Is there life out there? Sadly, discussion is precluded as to whether intelligent life permeates the media, or anything other than greed hangs in the polluted air breathed in by those mysterious entities periodically and enigmatically referred to as "investors."

Why truth should conform to institutional strictures on respectability, scientific manageability, profit potential or newsworthiness passes without comment, leaving behind a mood of dull intellectual caution and stupor. This has not happened overnight. Whereas scientifically minded psychologists now regularly chase the news, just a few decades ago students could study psychology, theoretically at least, as an arts-based discipline and seriously engage in philosophical and existential contemplation of the vicissitudes of life, love and reason. The insights of psychoanalysts of a variety of different hues – Freud, Jung, Bowlby, Reich, Fromm, Winnicott, Laing, to name but a few – were open to contemplation. From the earlier years of the twentieth century and at least into the 1960s and 1970s – even if by then on the margins of the discipline – one felt entitled to grapple with the intangible problems of human existence, pose questions about the two-way street that links the individual and society, and interrogate the discipline and its methods. The freedom to address these larger questions permitted a more open and questioning relationship between the student and the subject matter. Much has since been lost. These were times when a place still existed for individual stories – where each tale could shine a light on the marvels and tragedies fashioned by the contingencies of life, where the multitude of feelings and meanings woven into the text burst out and made common cause with the life and times of the reader. Nineteenth-century psychology closed with William James' *Principles of Psychology* and Freud's nascent steps into the murky depths of the unconscious. In these works human feelings, desires and foibles occupied the centre stage of psychology.

As the curtain came down on the twentieth century, narrative flow had given way to the stagnant waters of statistical and experimental prose, Freud had been relegated to a sideshow – outlawed, rarely performed, seldom advertised and reliant on a crew of ill-informed academic players barely able to remember the lines. The "everyday struggle to maintain integrity" (Starosta, 2007, p.163) and the search for universal themes in the particulars of a single life disappeared into a labyrinth of enforced forgetfulness. This was the "decade of the brain" – and the scarcity of the soul, sponsored with billions corporate dollars – the collection of one's neural matter having supplanted the psyche, which most psychologists had by then ceased to believe in. At one university I worked in, undergraduate students were informed at their induction that they were "not here to study the soul." Many seemed satisfied with the behavioural substitute on offer – but many I suspect were left with a profound disappointment. As the new century dawned psychologists had become convinced that neuroscience is not only the way to rescue the world from human folly, but also the sure-fire way to solve the mystery of being.

The malaise which besets contemporary scientifically minded psychology has scarcely registered amongst the majority of its practitioners. This may have something to do with the ongoing exclusion of such human preoccupations as justice, democracy, purpose, feeling and love – not to mention the everyday business of getting through the day – from its impersonal lexicon. It is also closely connected with the fact that the art and practice of reflecting on the nature of what is practised is seldom encouraged or engaged with. Psychology assumes and institutionalises the primacy of (cognitive) representation over action in all matters that are supposedly relevant and that it thinks we ought to know. But this one assumption, like most assumptions, is never put to the test. While science as a social institution has received increasing attention from sociologists of knowledge – rarely to the pleasure of scientific practitioners, it must be said – psychology as such an institution has received none. Without this we are poorly placed to understand how its functions, practices and "products," as well as its aims, both reflect and affect the wider society of which we are a part, and how it has progressively transformed public as well as private knowledge of self, the world and others. Understanding of the political economy of psychology (Roberts, 2015) and its relations with other social institutions (e.g. education, publishing, defence, law, medicine) needs to be augmented by an appreciation of its epistemological and moral transformative power. To engage in such an undertaking one need not accept as a prerequisite the self-proclaimed unity of the discipline.

The many divisions within academic psychology can give the impression that there is little but the name to hold the floundering whole together, and afford little or no opportunity to reflect on what the whole actually is – if it is anything at all beyond a discursive deception, a linguistic fiction drowning in a sea of ideological emptiness. Most academics spend the entirety of their careers knowing little or nothing about what their colleagues do. This is encouraged by the culture of academic specialism and reinforced by the increasingly impersonal nature of psychology which can find no space for human interest. The cultivated image of what psychology now is carries the imprimatur and seal of corporate approval. Just as movie-goers were not so long ago instructed that Matt Damon *is* Jason Bourne, since the cognitive revolution we are told psychology *is* now neuroscience. Neuroscience however is *not* psychology nor as coherent as a Bourne film. The dominance of this approach carries the thinly veiled mechanistic veneer of a new authoritarian or totalitarian aesthetic – the human information-processing ballet in which man and woman are remade as machine[2] – a "representational perversion" (Guéry & Deleule, 2014, p.103). It is a makeover many might not like if applied to themselves. The phantasmagorical ghost, guarding the secret of being, has been exorcised, left to roam the wild open spaces of public and poetic imagination, discarded from the psychological machine. The soul is the remit of the poet, the computational brain the remit of the scientist. Social science has undertaken the journey from Marcuse's one-dimensional man to zero-dimensional machine – all avenues beyond critical thought and the humanistic imperative squeezed from reality. But is this such a good idea? Is something not lost in the failure to embrace what poetry can tell us? Freud's psychology in James Hillman's eyes had been founded upon the poetic basis of the mind – not easy to reconcile with our contemporary faith in a coming scientific utopia. We may ask whether enlightenment only embraces the rational linear mind. And if so, is this enlightenment at all? The idea that a person is essentially a machine is a fantasy – but a fantasy seldom recognised as such.

Behind the clockwork make-believe lurks a disdain for and

fear of the time-limited nature of our bodily existence and a palpable and unseemly craving to extinguish what is recognisably human on the road to cybernetic and bio-computational immortality. Psychology continues to build promises on the premise that fundamental psychological processes exist that can be isolated, identified and controlled outside of any discernible context in which human beings find themselves and seek to understand their predicament. Under the guiding hand of this fantasy our conception of the machine has evolved from a metallic to an organic-synthetic hybrid. This is an aesthetic built not upon a love of human nature, but a contempt for it. The result is free of the complexities of gender, class, culture or history. Similarly our desires for what a well-functioning society looks like shift imperceptibly from the chaotic and free toward the ordered and determined, in harmony with the increasing top-down corporate command-control abolition of autonomy and democracy. Big Business and the press tell what us what to think and the academy responds in kind on its way to what Terry Eagleton described as a "slow death" at the hands of global capitalism. It ought to be considered odd that as science fiction plays with these tropes, the brutalities of the economic cycle rarely feature in the utopian and dystopian visions of the future – as if even in our worst imaginings we have developed a sensibility beyond greed and evaded the inevitabilities of boom and bust.

A further oddity is that as acceptance of this scientific myth has seeped further into our cultural consciousness, writers, artists and filmmakers have continuously explored the philosophical, ethical and dramatic possibilities of intelligent, self-cognisant machines being embodied with emotions – recognising as they have done so the possibility that emotion is an intelligible, necessary and perhaps inevitable response to the challenges of life, rooted in the physical embodiment of consciousness. Being conscious, one is always necessarily aware of one's physical existence in the world and with it actual and potential changes in one's state precipitated by change in the world. That is, being aware brings with it a *feeling* of being aware. Feelings, therefore, inhabit the boundary spaces between self and not self and by virtue of this *action*, elude and resist scientific representation. For the artist questions of meaning, feeling and purpose are intrinsic to such possibilities of being. They are not explained away simply because the substrate of their being is an embodied one. So it is that as art has sought to imbue machines with emotions, scientists have sought to expunge them. In Ridley Scott's *Blade Runner*, the android "replicants" are even described by their makers as "more human than human" – an uncanny recognition that we are becoming "less than human" as we head into the future. Psychologists are among the chief culprits of this vanishing trick. But who then should we say is dealing most appropriately with reality – the artist who accepts an undeniable facet of it or the would-be scientist who, in the interests of simplicity, control and reductionist explanation, does not? And if we choose the artist – what then do we mean by science, once its connection with reality has been severed?

Maybe psychology has become too popular and too influential for its own good. Maybe like Narcissus it has become enchanted by its own reflection, coming to see itself as so successful and legitimate an enterprise that there no longer exists any need for professional scepticism or introspection. As this hubris has grown, it has been joined by a collective amnesia clouding the consciousness with which daily work is undertaken. Instead of a re-membering of the assortment of critical attacks launched against the mechanisation of humanity over the years and sober reflection upon its dubious past, what we have is a dis-membering of this past. Not so much a re-construction of what has gone before, as an act of isolating and destroying its remaining constituent elements... suitable preparation for researching the void. Billig (2008) provides a fascinating summary of this exorcism of inconvenient history and the interests it serves but provides no antidote for it. As technical specialism grows, he argues, memory grows shorter.

Amongst the critical works ejected into the wilderness we may find Szasz's libertarian crusade against the intellectual, philosophical and moral shortcomings of psychiatry and psychology; Kelly's pragmatic attempt to transform psychology into the study of the person; Laing's similarly determined efforts to mould psychiatry, psychology and psychotherapy into a human science theoretically supported by existentialism and Marxism; European social psychologists' exhumation of the "crisis" in experimental social psychology; and Foucault's positioning of psychology as a new force in disciplinary social control. In recent years these critiques have been joined by Smail's dissection of the anatomy of power (and its denial) in psychological theory and practice; Kagan's lament for the lack of discernible context in most psychological research; Parker's exposé of the ideological nature of psychology; and Itten and Roberts' consideration of the neoliberal influence pervading the discipline. This has made psychology not merely a theoretically enslaved accomplice to the promotion of capitalist realism, a willing and able assistant to the mercenary society (Hutton, 2015) with a haunting presence at the scene of many political and military crimes, but also a contributor in large part to its divorce from everyday reality. The self-congratulatory neglect of all this comes at a considerable cost. The wholesale denial of these critiques and the daily "business as usual" approach in the psychological mainstream have had an enormous effect in shaping our ideas about the kind of problems we face and what the most effective means are for bringing about personal and social change. As for our salvation, this has never been on the scientific priestly agenda. We are already damned.

For neoliberal positivistic psychology to have weathered these storms might lead one to presuppose that what is on offer is a healthy, robust and well-grounded conceptualisation of the person. This is the view of the outsider before they cross the threshold and take up membership of the psychology club. After a suitable period of assimilation – deemed to be three years, but effectively over in one or two – the belief that psychology is about understanding people *as people* is erased. However, despite this erasure, vestiges of the assorted critiques, each in their own way, linger on in the stubborn subterranean ruins of the intellectual archive and hint at fundamental shortcomings in what now constitutes the dominant psychological tradition. Psychology – not for the first time in its relatively short life – has entered a critical state; but it is a crisis which is denied. The assorted strangled voices highlight the neglect of both human experience and the very conditions of human life in which experience and behaviour occur – the vital ingredients which Hillman and Benjamin in their own ways map out as indispensable for under-standing the human situation. The succession of moments lived, whose sum total for each of us constitutes the content of a human life, thus remain neglected, arousing neither passion nor wonder in the minds of the majority who now practise what is called psychology. Passion, wonder, puzzlement, confusion, boredom; the entirety of emotional life, in fact, is largely absent. Practitioners are advised that work proceeds best from an Archimedean, emotion-free zone. But the "'unclouded' 'innocent eye'" as Walter Benjamin (2007, p.85) knew, has long since been "a lie" and even a measure of "incompetence." The absence of passion exists in parallel to a dual commitment to obey the imperatives of organisational psychology's avowed political neutrality whilst simultaneously responding "on automatic" to the totalising servo-control directives issued from the bunkers by corporate movers and shakers, "vice chancellors who behave as though they are running General Motors" (Eagelton, 2015), and their dutifully obedient minions who comprise the managerial class in higher education. The orders require academics to put making money ahead of thinking for oneself whether in the guise of writing, developing minds or producing knowledge. In this new business environment, writing books is considered a vulgar obstacle to making money; students have adapted to it by not reading them.

The quality of education delivered under this cloud can now be considered as a form of debasement not dissimilar to pornography – corrupt, depraved and difficult to define. The multiplication of league tables and the ethos of competition that pervades the academy means that academics are under increasing pressure to ensure pass rates approach the ceiling – and beyond that the sky. This happens despite the poor attendance on many courses; students now being too busy working to actually attend the courses for which their jobs are paying. Non-attendance is no impediment to achievement as pass rates soar in order to "produce" satisfaction levels which the management believes will maintain their place (and their faith) in the league tables. A reality looms which is not far from the fictional totalitarian "learning" system depicted in the surreal TV series *The Prisoner*. In this, a new educational experiment promised a three-year course in three minutes, 100% pass rates guaranteed. All parroting the same litany of facts, the "successful" students were incapable of independent thought. Maybe one of the points being made by Patrick McGoohan, the architect of the series, was that organised education and captivity were birds of a feather, with the dialects of freedom and slavery endlessly caught in the slipstream. For anyone currently labouring or "schooled" under the manufactured glare of neoliberal higher education this truth is difficult to avoid. A letter signed by over a hundred academics in the *Guardian* in July 2015[3] described the situation as one in which: "innovation, creativity, originality and critical thought, as well as notions of social justice [are] being threatened by forces of marketisation demanding 'competitiveness' and 'efficiency' in teaching and research." This, they went on to say, "generates continuous pressures to standardise, conform, obey and duplicate in order to be 'transparent' to measurement." What the authors do not explicitly say, but insinuate, is that the "obsession with measurement" is ultimately about preservation of the social order – a neoliberal social order which requires levels of surveillance unprecedented in human history. It is no coincidence that at a time when the UK government is described by one of its own MPs as adopting the tactics of General Franco,[4] the *Guardian* newspaper features regular articles by "Academics Anonymous," freedom of speech in academia having shifted from being a right to a covert thrill – indulged in while looking over one's shoulder. With "measurement" everywhere both literal and metaphoric, genuine scholarly activity increasingly moves underground – a clandestine pastime rolled out in the sanctity of one's own private bolthole.

Measurement entails that numbers are to be assigned to everyone and everything in the higher-education universe in tandem with the demand that we "measure up" to the harsh reality of a cut-throat business world of competition and selfishness. The cost alluded to above therefore is at once both political and moral. But it is also intellectual and emotional. The stifling of initiative, creativity and critical thought are nothing but the hallmarks of a psychology which has been moulded over generations by the demands of capital, and which has now come to resemble a commercial enterprise in more ways than its adherents would care to admit. In accord with this the discipline has functioned to depoliticise social space. The principal means by which it has achieved this, has involved the theoretical interiorising of a variety of social, historical and economic relations which express the logic of industrial capitalism – resilience, hardiness, intelligence and vitality as individual counterpoints to unsuccessful collective subordination. Positioning the "forces" driving human behaviour as individual and private, rather than social and public, neutralises the imperatives and prospects for addressing the social and political problems of the neglected real world (Roberts, 2015).

For Guéry and Deleule (2014) survival is the real refrain of contemporary psychology. They argue that its research program is actually concerned with the individual's Darwinian struggle for survival in the midst of a mechanical-technological monster (industrial capitalism) dependent upon what Foucault would describe as human bio-power. With this emphasis on individual survival, Guéry and Deleule argue that psychology fulfils its ideological destiny – as "a seemingly indispensable gear in the social machinery"[5] (2014, p.114), it atomises the social and at a stroke de-contextualises and individualises the challenges of existence. Thus, beneath the psychological froth, the real entity whose survival lies at the centre of modern psychology is the capitalist behemoth, parasitic as it is on not merely human bio-power but the global planetary eco-system. The danger with parasites, as any biologist well knows, is that they sometimes destroy their host. Marx argued that its imperatives destroy everything in its path – "all that is solid melts into air"; little wonder that he asked whether ultimately it will destroy itself.

What the neoliberal psychological environment demands in order to conceal these broader truths is a fundamentally dishonest means of inquiry. In Dr Johnson's view, London in the eighteenth century had become a landscape "transformed" by those in power "into a festering repository of corrupt practices" (Beaumont, 2016, p.220). The same descriptive richness could equally be applied to much in the repertoire of contemporary psychological "science." Here thrives a pretence that what the dutifully obedient academic does, from an intellectual stand-point, arises not from the internalised strategic logic of the corporate university adrift in a dog-eat-dog capitalist matrix, but from the purest of pure motives of scientific curiosity. A case of Big Business washes whiter. That many players in the academic game profess this, and appear to believe it, only indicates how deep the sleep is into which they have descended. Unconscious and alienated, firstly from their own authentic human possibilities and secondly the world of business real politic in which academia now resides, few dare look outside the laboratory to tell the tale of human behaviour. When Winnicott (1986) waxed lyrically on the ubiquity of the "false self" he countered any undue pessimism by remarking that every individual reserved at least one area of their life for special treatment – a space where there was no room for compromise with society's demands for compliance. Increasingly, with the neoliberal hijacking of the academy (Giroux, 2014) along with the commercialisation of private life, this space has retreated from public view. Disobedience and rebellion have been privatised, the "conservative status quo mentality" is the in-thing, and the daily grind dispenses on-the-job training in passivity (see Glaser, 2015).

With the desire to challenge the status quo repressed into the scientific and artistic unconscious, a good many behavioural scientists function as little more than ancillary management robots – administrative cyborgs – espousing the higher-education bureaucratic management newspeak *as if* they really had to. It is worth stressing that they do not. Whether psychologists, schooled in their own brand of individualism, may be particularly prone to believing the cybernetic mantra that "resistance is futile" is anybody's guess, but there can be little doubt that academic psychology is now in servitude to the profit monster and functions as one of its chief weapons. Over the past few decades, the extending reach of psychological frameworks and modes of explanation into the public realm should be seen alongside the escalating social breakdown, poverty, criminality and atomisation of labour power which has accompanied the development of neoliberal capitalism over the same time period (Mason, 2015). They are not unrelated, psychology perversely providing a plausible theoretical cover for individual action while the systematic ransacking of the social order proceeds at breakneck pace. As a consequence of this role it also perpetuates the mental dynamic played out between exploiters and exploited, each believing their respective roles are solely a function of their own personalities, motivations and reason.

The destruction of free thinking in our universities under the auspices of public accountability and market friendliness can only be to the detriment of any genuine attempt to wrestle with the exigencies of earthly existence. The challenge to live well and the moral and practical wisdom that might enable it – Aristotle's *"phronesis"* – have disappeared off the radar; missing in action one could say, but it might be nearer the truth to say that what is missing in our quest to live well is action. The age-old desire to unearth/uncover/discover the meaning of life is born of a misapprehension that the desired "holy grail" can be represented – literally re-presented back to us – in a form convenient and amenable to language and logic. The contemporary mass-produced myth of the good life, which has been gathering pace since the industrial revolution, is that this comprises comfort and consumption – a passive hedonistic accommodation to the mores of a consumer society, exemplified in Huxley's *Brave New World*. But what it is that we truly desire cannot be bought or consumed – it is the living of one's life selflessly, as a form of action that opens up, reverberates and resonates beyond one's self. This is an art transmissible only by example, recognised in feeling, learnt by trial, failure and error. It is not a matter of reason and rationality. In a culture obsessed with winning at all costs and "elite" performance, that which is potentially nearby moves far away. An old Zen parable captures something of the flavour of this (see Hyman, 1982, p.87). A young boy wishing to study martial arts asks the master, "How long must I study?" "Ten years at least," replies the master. "Ten years is a long time," says the boy, "What if I studied twice as hard as all other students?" "Twenty years," intones the master. "But what if I practice day and night with all my effort?" pleads the boy. "Thirty years," comes the reply. That which is sought cannot be found, at least not by the methods taught in our universities and filling the pages of countless textbooks.

Over the course of my long association with behavioural science, I cannot recall the concept of virtue ever being discussed nor have I encountered it in any psychological text. Human vices have on the other hand received plentiful treatment, from being rationalised as evolutionary predispositions to being championed as successful decision-making stratagems in the emerging new "decision" science. The focus of convenience is, unsurprisingly, business and economic decision-making; the uncertainties of virtue sacrificed for the certainties of vice. This is necessary for us to remain pessimistic about change. To make a revolution, to turn the wheel, to undertake the painstaking work against social inertia one has to believe in a world beyond the given. So in place of a psychology that strives to examine and cultivate virtue (for example dependability, honesty, courage, justness, responsibility, resistance) in the face of the unseemly world order we inhabit, what we see is a discipline that has organised its activities in response to the libidinous wishes of the powerful to manipulate and control behaviour. The desired pathways toward this embrace the regulation of states of mind and the development of technologies in service to this end – marketing, face recognition, weaponry, artificial intelligence, pharmacology and propaganda being but a few. The resultant psychology perforce shuns any notion of intentionality or freedom and proceeds on the basis that absolutely everything is explicable – with a fear rather than a celebration of the human mystery and no space for the unknown beyond a quantifiable statistical notion of residual error variance.

The journey to our current predicament has been long and haphazard, but there seems little prospect that the collective community of psychologists are going to step off the moving walkway any day now, even if headed for the cliff edge. However, what is becoming increasingly clear is that the current preferred model for doing psychology – Big Science programs in genetics, machine intelligence and psychopharmacology, funded by corporations and government – is not going to produce the good life or a good life for anyone who is not beholden to the movement of share prices. In many ways the malaise into which the entire discipline has fallen can be found in microcosm in psychology's relationship to the issues of conflict, war and peace. Psychology, of course, seeks to understand human behaviour but as it grows in importance its role in creating and generating behaviour grows in tandem. Our understanding and theorising of social conflict draw heavily on experimental work deriving from Henri Tajfel's social-identity theory. What is seldom, if ever, said is that this work is entirely lacking in ecological validity – laboratory studies with small numbers of individuals simply have no bearing on real-world conflict situations where very often tens of thousands of people, including military personnel, members of armed militia, representatives of the media, corporate financiers and members of the general public, are engaged in complex social interactions – which include concrete "interactions" with weapons as well as more abstract ones with local, cultural and historically situated knowledge.

The elephant in the room in our obsession with theory is that no social psychological theory has ever predicted any real-world conflict. One can think of the ongoing drama in the Ukraine and the breakup of the former Yugoslavia in the 1990s as two examples, but really, any will suffice. I will go as far as to say that no matter how far into the future one journeys, no large-scale conflict will *ever* be predicted by social psychological theory. Despite this obvious problem[6] it is heresy to admit that such events on the ground are driven by larger social forces, for psychology is insistent that psychological events must always be moved by extant knowable psychological forces. Because of this it lives in a self-enclosed world, a retreat from the real, yet inviting and luring legions of the public to join it there. It is an invitation and a temptation that must be resisted. As an institution, social psychology functions on the premise that everything possible in the social world must already be explicable. Thus, not only does psychology, once it has donned the magic cloak of scientific respectability, assume that the world is knowable, but it is also practiced as if the world is already fundamentally known! If this were actually true it would suggest a number of things: firstly, that psychology has now reached a state of epistemological advancement that no science has ever come close to achieving, or could ever hope to achieve even in principle; secondly, that the creativity and ingenuity of (human) nature is constrained in such a way that it can introduce no new phenomenon that is not already understandable within the confines of existing knowledge; and thirdly, this state of theoretical omniscience would actually undermine the point of doing any research at all. In sum this dogmatic posturing reflects a serious deficiency once again in how the discipline approaches the real world. What can we say when on the one hand we have Albert Einstein declaring that the human mind, no matter how highly trained, cannot grasp the universe, and on the other hand we have social psychologists routinely declaring that the world as it exists already fits into what the scarcely-one-hundred-year-old science has come up with. This juxtaposition of opinion ought to give us something to think about.

The relegation of the real beneath the instruments of professional power occurs not just with theory but also with method, where throughout the discipline, preferred Big Data processing methods (multivariate statistical analysis, DNA sequencing and analysis, MRI scanning, to name but three) have become a byword for truth, as if the sheer complexity of a given procedure – now to be considered a form of professional power – somehow guarantees not only the validity of any claim made on the basis of it, but also its immunity from criticism. Oliver James' (2014) comments, on the spurious claims made by psychiatrists regarding the putative role of genetic factors in mental ill health, illustrate how particular professional groups take such immunity for granted.

The theoretical, philosophical and methodological problems connected with our attempts to turn human behaviour into a field of interacting variables are complemented by our professional willingness – despite our professed neutrality and alleged freedom from bias – to actively aid those forces of state which all too often manufacture war. Personnel selection, psychological operations (PSYOPS), enhanced interrogation (torture) techniques, surveillance, ergonomics, missile guidance and artificial intelligence are just some of the ways in which psychologists have become front-line staff in the bludgeoning of liberty and the commission of death and destruction. The recent failure of the American Psychological Association (APA) to discipline one of their members, John Leso, for ethical violations after he had admitted taking part in the effective torture of Mohammed Al-Qahtani at Guantanamo Bay indicates the magnitude of organisational complicity in state-sponsored violence. Under the direction of its ethics chief, Stephen Behnke, the organisation recast APA's guidelines to be more open to torture techniques. An independent investigation by US attorney David Hoffman also found that many more APA members had lied and covered up their role in the torture of detainees.[7] The state-sponsored violence in question, it must be remembered, was a sub-routine in the multinational corporate acquisition of Iraq's oil reserves.

Many aspects of the above problems are a product of psychology's ill-suited endeavour to masquerade as a science and to seek state and corporate authorisation and sponsorship to alleviate its scientific inferiority complex. The nature and degree of psychology's co-option by such powers signals an important moment in the development of contemporary capitalism. It is as if without such control of our internal mental processes, continuation of the economic exploitation game would be in question.

That beneath the apparent display of overwhelming power lies a barely concealable vulnerability to obsolescence and decay. As the self-sustaining dynamic of capitalism now ultimately depends on the manipulation of mind – so that seeing is no longer tantamount to believing – everything else we had believed in as the fruits of the great modernist project threaten to disintegrate: democracy, peace, academic freedom, the welfare state, Western hegemony and even reality itself, which Baudrillard (2008), after Nietzsche, declared has already been murdered. If the present is not safe then neither the past nor the future can be guaranteed. Our once-confident visions of future technological and scientific utopias seem ready to morph at a moment's notice into dystopian nightmares. Culturally this is evident at every turn: Even Hollywood, bereft of ideas, now endlessly recycles the successes of yesteryear, its sci-fi dreams locked into a decaying nostalgia for the future. This is exemplified tragi-technologically in the digital reanimation of a 1980s Jeff Bridges alongside his present-day self in the 3D extravaganza *Tron: Legacy* released in 2010. In 2015, we find an ageing Arnold Schwarzenegger locking horns with his younger digitally reconstructed double in *Terminator: Genisys*. As with *Tron*, what is at stake is the ephemerality of our past vision (our memories) of the future, but the *Terminator* franchise also hints at a radical threat to our own sense of temporality. We are no longer sure where exactly we came from or where we are going. As the newly remodelled character of Sarah Connor shouts, "Everything's changed." If the past and the future are no longer what they once were – how can the present contain any stability? But if the current order is so unstable then in actuality the possibilities for change open up – including the multiple possibilities for a radical and more humane restructuring of social reality rooted in a reinvention of the critical project of modernity. Psychology has thus become the Panglossian instrument of economic power to contain this threat and to convince us that nothing is amiss after all, that "all is for the best in the best of all possible worlds." In all of these possible worlds we are supposed to see capitalism triumphant. It is incumbent upon us to remember that not all drama follows a preordained script.

The exit roads from such dangerous ways are far from obvious but paradoxically a good place to start might be an admission that we don't really know what to do – that the past has not furnished us with the necessary tools to escape the terra incognita of thought and practice. Ferguson (2016) sees psychology as an enterprise trapped inside an ill-designed web of scientific mythmaking, struggling to escape accusations of pseudoscience. Unfortunately, while the diagnosis has merit, his view as to how we should escape from this follows the same well-worn path that led us into it in the first place – the quest that we should pursue "objective" science. Aware that one is in a fable, what narratives can we turn to in order to remake reality?

The future that beckons asks that we relinquish all of our claims to expertise, knowledge, certainty and authority and, with these, any lately acquired habits of time-keeping. This is an assuredly unfamiliar stance for academics but would allow the springs of co-creation to arise from the depths of ignorance, in particular from toleration of the uncertainty of ignorance and the temporality of ignorance: we would need to linger there a moment longer than is comfortable and then some more. While freedom can never be slavery, nor war peace, our ignorance, if acknowledged, can be a source of strength and vitality, an opportunity for renewal. Necessity is the mother of invention… a step at a time being the only viable response to conditions of uncertainty, a third way for moving not forward nor backward but sideways, neither confronting nor obeying the diktats of authority.

Several viable and inter-related avenues of exploring the unknown can be considered. What these have in common is a desire to reach beyond the accepted cultural myths of psychology furnished by neoliberal Big Science, to decouple it from its institutional moorings and rebuild the practice and performance of psychology from the ground up. One avenue is to sidestep the scientist-practitioner model developed in clinical psychology and re-seek psychology's roots as an art. Another is to approach psychology's place in community life, work and activism. Rather than seeing the field as a place to develop theory we can contemplate it as a place where we seek to destroy it, where we seek to discover and relearn, perhaps for the first time, how to effectively tackle social and individual problems on the ground – to cultivate a practical, knowing art of resistance. We may find that human psychology is deeply important in this but we don't have to assume it nor assume that any effective action will necessarily start from there. If we are serious and/or indeed playful about this – the two are after all not incompatible – psychologists can abandon their claims to omniscience (and omnipotence) whilst being mindful of a range of possible public responses to a new-found anti-expertise: distrust, disappointment, disillusionment, bewilderment are just a few, though in the UK at least, one can also include the fog of anti-intellectual thought which saturates the cultural air. And finally we can go back to our own beginnings as human beings – entrants to a potentially enchanting world of human warmth, love, wonder and mystery – the principle enigmas of our existence while we breathe. "Life," in the words of Laurie Anderson, "is a team sport."

Too much of theory is premised on the trauma and cataclysm of our entry into the world and what might terribly unfold in it; little or none is devoted to its magic and awe. The mysterious encompasses more than the mere fact of the unpredictability of the world; it is what is grasped by our awareness of the specific and total nature of being as enigmatic, unfathomable and strange, aided by the continuing unknown we confront on a daily basis in all our contingent dealings with other people and events. As physicist Lee Smolin (Unger & Smolin, 2015) acknowledged, dealing with it is not a matter for science – but whether it is celebrated, ignored or feared, the riddle of being lies at the heart of our existence and is therefore not just a metaphysical issue but an existential and psychological one. Existence is uncanny.

These opening remarks suggest another vision for the discipline is possible and one of the intentions behind this work is to explore this possibility. The present book has emerged from several previous assessments – first of all, of events in which psychology has played a major role (e.g. the war in Iraq and the War on Terror); secondly, the cultural role of psychology in promoting images of human nature, distress and recovery; and thirdly, a critical look at the political, economic and ideological context that has shaped the history and development of psychology.

These had led me to conclude that, from a humanistic and emancipatory point of view, psychology, much like the existing economic order, has reached an impasse, perhaps even a dead end; that in contemporary brain science we may already be witnessing the intellectual ruins of the psychological future, the rubble on which will be found the failed answers to the questions of our existence. The logical question then arose as to whether psychology was an enterprise which ought to be abandoned in its entirety or whether some form of reimagining of the art and science of the soul was possible, one which could simultaneously reinvigorate our understanding of what it means to be human and permit an escape from the clutches of decadent orthodoxy. This need not mean the entire psychological community be tarnished with the same brush or that the complete canon of psychological knowledge be consigned to the scrap heap – indeed islands of what we might call hopeful practice can still be found in both social psychology and the mental health field. However these islands alone – still tied to the empirical and epistemological mind-set that animates the rest of the discipline, and facing as they do the rising tide of corporate pressure – are unlikely to provide a sufficient basis for any new kind of approach. The time is ripe therefore to nurture, incubate and embark upon the acts of imagination that will determine whether other very different kinds of psychology or non-psychology are possible and viable. But there is also the question of whether we need to invent the new to escape the old. In psychotherapy it is sometimes recognised that in order to go on, once must go back – in our case to the discarded, the neglected, the overlooked, the unrecognised – the psychologies that lie off the beaten track, "off-world." They hover on the hazy boundaries of cultures, practices and disciplines, a cloud of virtual possibilities to aid us in the pursuit of integrity, then and now. The official history traces a line of inheritance from Wundt's laboratory, through the fields of classical and operant conditioning to the clear light of the cognitive revolution. I believe that this narrative is neither linear nor inevitable and certainly not true. Many vibrant and different notions of how to grapple with the human condition have been overlooked and at times forcefully removed from sight. We need to open a space for these counterfactual psychologies to breathe the investigative air once again.

The arguments throughout the rest of this book are intended to cultivate, explore and play with a variety of means for crossing/straddling the variegated borders of the psyche – between the known and unknown, the individual and social, the lived and imagined, the life we live and the life we might have lived, the scientific and non-scientific, the disappearing now of past, present and future time. Reality contains the psychological but does not privilege it. Accordingly we require a vision that contains but does not privilege psychological explanation and that positions psychological work as art and practice in the world in which we live. Is this a multidisciplinary approach to the enduring strangeness of the human condition? Is it a side-step into contrary disciplines and practices, an off-road into intel-lectual Badlands, a radical critical perspective – a "what-if" psychology? Is it an attempt to escape the punitive institutional border patrols of academia? Is a psychology that is not psychology possible?

There is no pilot
Jump out of the plane
– Laurie Anderson

Two

From Alienation to Estrangement

All aspects of the human condition are somehow related to politics
– Hannah Arendt (1998, p.7)

...truth is relational, not relative
– Svetlana Boym (2010, p.67)

Resistance is the secret of joy
– Alice Walker (cited in Solnit, 2014, p.230)

If we are to make headway in developing an alternative kind of psychology, one which gives due deference to both context and experience, then we will need to examine those intellectual frameworks that are both available and viable for such a project. Only then may we be able to fashion a new kind of approach to the human situation. One of the neglected aspects of contemporary psychology (Itten & Roberts, 2014) concerns the nature of human experience in the world; how we as people, each of us a unique living embodiment of our total life experience, engage with and are engaged by the overarching political system/society of which we are a part. This relationship between the personal and the wider environmental and socio-cultural-political realm can be considered the core problem of the social sciences in so far as it attempts to comprehend the nature of the human condition. As such it is integral to the social construction of reality and how we understand social phenomena. It will form the subject matter of this chapter as I review three key approaches – from Marx, Foucault and Boym – which may directly inform the contextual and political nature of our experience. These three approaches, dealing respectively with alienation, subjectivity and estrangement, have been proposed by three quite different theorists, each of whom emphasises the importance of contextualising our experience in a human world which is at once social, cultural and historical in its nature.

Karl Marx

Considerable confusion still surrounds Marx's place in the social sciences – this is due in some small part to the confusion which surrounds the understanding of Marxism and its relationship to the communist movements of the twentieth century. Fear of the political content of Marx's ideas has resulted in their almost complete exclusion from mainstream psychological thought, which has largely adopted an avowedly apolitical, positivistic and ahistorical stance in its investigations of the human subject. Marxism is both a philosophy and a method of enquiry. It encompasses three aspects: firstly, a method of enquiry for the study of social processes; secondly, a theory of economics; and thirdly, a theory of historical change and development – historical materialism – erected on the intellectual platform constructed by Hegel. Whereas Hegel had given an account of the gradualist development of consciousness and knowledge, Marx, famously declaring that it was material conditions which determine human consciousness, endeavoured to provide a "lawful" explanation of historical development through a succession of antagonistic class relations.

What will concern us here will be, first of all, Marx's stress on the historical nature of human life, and secondly, the nature and quality of human experience at this moment of historical development under the prevailing capitalist system. The importance of framing psychological data within an historical context has of course been stressed by Gergen (1973) who considered the contingent nature of much psychological data – upon time, place and culture – rendered the discipline less suited to a perspective rooted in natural science and more to one rooted in history.

One of Marx's central arguments deals with the nature of human experience in our own historical époque. The relationship between the individual and the social lies at the heart of Marx's thought – indeed Marx considered it central to his entire political philosophy. In it the diminishing of human worth was no longer seen as a simple consequence of the exercise from on high of power "too great for wisdom or restraint" (Sophocles, 2008, p.77) but also, in part, of our own willing complicity. Marx's examination of the relationship between the individual and society led to what for him was a key question – "Why do we participate in our own oppression?" Marx believed he had the answer in his conceptions of alienation and mystification as forms of dislocation from an inherent human nature. Human nature was conceived by Marx not as the property of any given individual but as a characteristic of the human species, considered as a whole. In his view this nature was not a presently given fact but something to be realised (at a species level) through historically determined economic and political development which would free people from the chains of oppressive labour. As Hegel had sought to account for the perfection of ideas and spirit, Marx sought the perfection of humanity in the social and economic realm.

Alienation and Mystification

Alienation and mystification then were primarily considered as characteristic forms of group psychology, which were inevitable features of life in a socially stratified society where the means of production lay disproportionately in the hands of one class – the capitalists – to the detriment of the overwhelming majority of the population who were workers (actual or potential). In Marx's view both capitalist and worker were alienated from their fundamental humanity with the form of this alienation occurring in several distinct varieties; these are mediated through our relationships with the material world of manufactured objects, our relationships with the labour process, and our relationships with one another – these comprising together a set of mutually interlocking influences.

Arguably the most fundamental form of alienation that Marx addresses is the alienation from oneself whereby one loses the right to consider oneself the author/director of one's own actions. One can readily envisage this, as one behaviourally fulfils the wishes of one's employers from the vantage point of one's allotted place on the assembly line, or reads from the company script in the hot-house of a telephone centre, dutifully obeying the commands from on high to sell whatever one is in the business of selling to legions of unwilling customers. In advanced capitalist societies this kind of alienation has now filtered through to the so-called intellectual professions: computer programmers, for example, writing lines of code which will comprise a functional part of the operating system of machines designed to kill and maim; or academics forced to write endless business-friendly grant applications in order to secure a living from the corporate table or to fend off management harassment. From this it follows that one's ability to define the nature of one's relationship with other people and with one's work is similarly deleteriously affected. Capitalist social relations, as Eric Fromm so eloquently described, sees other people also turned into things. Our capacity to act fully autonomously, creatively and in accordance with an emotional desire to treat others well is transformed under the conditions of the omnipresent market into programmed rather than creative activity. This not only eats into the possibility of engaging with work in a way which is psychologically satisfying, but separates us from any say in how the products of our work are to be used.

Alienation from ourselves and our work is compounded by the forward march of technology. As Marx noted, industrial production is organised to suit the work of machines and within such a system the human worker becomes ancillary to the machine – a cog in the clockwork manufacture of commodities for use and want, but not need. From this it is a logical development that we ourselves come increasingly to resemble machines. Not only are we theorised and objectified under contemporary systems of scientific representation to be nothing other than biological and biochemical machines, but there is also the matter of how our daily activities, characteristics, propensities, foibles, creative works and thoughts – our very private lives in fact – are now sold on the open market as entertainment. We all thus risk a fate of de facto commoditisation.

From the Marxist perspective then it is not only individuals who can be alienated but entire collectives. Let me illustrate by way of a brief story. A friend of mine, a respected academic at another university, recently explained to me how he had been chastised by university managers. For his sins, while moving office, he had taken it upon himself to transport a couple of grey filing cabinets. These, it transpired, had now been outlawed and declared non-filing cabinets under the university's new corporate colour-branding scheme. White was in, grey was out. Tucker (2012, p.118) bemoaned the way in which "[t]he centrally managed university" has become "a parody of a university, a Potemkin village that has the facade of a university […] devoted to the implementation of absurd, senseless, immoral, and harmful policies that percolate down through an anonymous, unaccountable bureaucratic hierarchy." When more attention is given to the colour branding of office furniture than actual scholarship, the university, if it actually exists as anything other than a simulacrum, has become alienated from itself.

These fundamental psychological and social psychological constructs of Marx have occupied a distinct niche in strands of psychoanalytic thought. Fromm and Laing may be considered two of the more noteworthy contributors to this. Highly relevant to the project of producing a more relevant and encompassing form of psychology, both are now largely unknown to most students of psychology.

Eric Fromm

Fromm has probably been foremost among the psychoanalytic fraternity to make use of Marx's insights. Fromm, who could lay claim to being the first political psychologist[8], argued that in both Marx's early (*The Economic and Philosophical Manuscripts*) and later works (*Capital*) there was a treasure trove of hopes and insights for students of the human character. He considered Marx a humanist, who portrayed the human character as pregnant with possibilities. Fromm considered Marx's concept of alienation fundamental for understanding contemporary human malaise – perverting, as he saw it, our understanding of life, love and labour. He argued (Fromm, 1995, 2013) that personal and social relations and notably gender relations throughout society have become enslaved to the operations of the market. These have produced in their turn a mentality which has contributed to a shift in social relationships away from norms of solidarity, mutuality and community to ones based on manipulation and instrumentality. He thus contrasted two modes of existence struggling for the spirit of humankind. On the one hand was a "being mode" concerned with love – conceived as an art, a "self-renewing and self-increasing" (2013, p.39) interpersonal creative capacity which was nor primarily about one's relationship to a specific individual but was "an *attitude, an orientation of character* which determines the relatedness of a person to the world as a whole" (1995, p.36). The extent to which this mode was prevalent in society – as with other characterological and psychological propensities – could be understood by careful description and analysis of human behaviour under prevailing social conditions. Opposed to the being mode was the "having mode." This was a mode of living concerned with acquiring material possessions, money and power. Its bedfellows were aggression, greed, envy and violence. Fromm's background in psychoanalysis saw these psychological responses to the material conditions of the day as attempts to solve fundamental issues of autonomy and separateness from others with which we must grapple from our earliest days.

Fromm's ideas have continuing relevance for us, as – like Gergen – he situated human life within the given conditions of its existence. He recognised that these conditions carried considerable implications not just for the kinds of psychological knowledge we will produce but also how we go about acquiring and producing it. Like George Kelly, the personal construct theorist, he adopted a reflexive stance to psychological enquiry and lamented that "modern academic and experimental psychology" had to a large extent become "a science dealing with alienated man, studied by alienated investigators with alienated and alienating methods" (Fromm, 1973, p.69). Fromm was certainly not alone in appreciating how important Marx's ideas were for a truly critical variant of psychology and psychoanalysis. That job was also to fall to R.D. Laing, another psychoanalyst.

R.D. Laing

Laing without doubt took the idea of alienation much further than Fromm. It could be argued, however, that one of Fromm's insights could have been of immense use to Laing had he picked up on it. When Fromm (2004, p.101) wrote that "modern man believes himself to be motivated by self-interest and yet [...] actually his life is devoted to aims which are not his own," he was highlighting an issue that has considerable significance for the legitimacy we ascribe to the mental health system, notably the validity of its fundamental operating principles. These sentiments retain their capacity to disturb but they remain undiscussed within the psychological mainstream and rarely considered even on the periphery. To the extent that they languish in obscurity in the dusty corridors of psychology, as unemployed explanatory artifices, the discipline remains, as Nietzsche remarked, "a vice" (1968, p.23).

Fromm's observation raises questions about what happens when, instead of remaining unaware that one's actions might not in effect be primarily authored by oneself, one achieves a measure of insight into one's alienation. Herein lies a fundamental problem, central to the operation of the mental health system. Under current social norms one is not supposed to realise that one is alienated – that one performs actions authored elsewhere. If, in a moment of awareness, a person claims that they are a puppet merely responding mechanically and obediently to "alien" orders – or that their body is an empty shell controlled by external alien powers – they may well find themselves designated not in touch with reality but "out of it" and likely diagnosed with "paranoid schizophrenia." If the reality of the relationship that one's own actions have to the wider forces of power breaks through into consciousness and produces signs of observable distress, the chances of psychiatric incarceration are elevated still further. The possibility that such claims – statements expressing one's predicament – might actually be accurate descriptions, metaphorically speaking, of one's present relationship to the wider world and the dominant system of social and material relations, is simply not up for consideration.[9] That Laing realised this conundrum is evident from his comments in The Politics of the Family (1971, p.74) where he remarked: "They think anyone who wakes up, or who, still asleep, realizes that what is taken to be real is a 'dream' is going crazy." However, beyond poetic flourishes aimed at the barely awake society he saw surrounding him, Laing did not systematically explore this terrain as he might – declining for example to examine his vast archive of family data culled from interviews with families whose offspring had not entered the mental health system, due to what for him was its immensely boring nature (see Mullan, 1995).

Laing's most noteworthy contribution to knowledge arguably came not from his earlier existential-phenomenological analyses, but from his use of Marx's psychological insights, particularly his ground-breaking studies of the micro-politics of family life in which he employed Marx's concepts of alienation and mystification. Laing (1965, pp.344-5) described the latter as:

> *the substitution of false for true constructions of what is being experienced, being done (praxis), or going on (process), and the substitution of false issues for the actual issues [...] If we detect mystification, we are alerted to the presence of a conflict of some kind that is being evaded. The mystified person [...] is unable to see the authentic conflict [...] He may experience false peace, false calm, or inauthentic conflict and confusion over false issues.*

In Laing and Esterson's (1964) appropriation of the concept of mystification – in the course of their examination of family dynamics and what we problematically call mental health (Szasz, 2010) – the effects, though still propagated by means of group actions and internalised psychological processes, came to be more keenly felt in particular individuals. As Roberts and Hewer (2015) contend, Laing's analysis of the debilitating effects of mystification is applicable to any social system whatever its level of complexity – be this the family, the workplace or the community of nation states. They suggest three conditions are necessary for serious psychological distress to be produced within any social network. Firstly, that conflict occurs in which important roles and traditions are challenged or undermined. Secondly, that particular political manoeuvres and tactics in the face of this conflict are employed – not necessarily consciously – that aim to maintain or restore the desired status quo. These "political" tactics often involve the manipulation and control of memory; they may comprise the denial, mystification and invalidation of the experience of the members of the relevant social system (e.g. family members, co-workers, political dissidents) who are deemed responsible for disturbing the favoured axes of orientation together with a denial that their actions are indeed mystifying or invalidating of the experience of others. Thirdly, and crucial to the psychological well-being of anyone enmeshed in such a social system, is the absence of support or solidarity available from anyone else inside the system to facilitate opposition to these operations. Thus individuals are rendered alone, confused and uncertain about what is real and what is not.

As an example one can consider the current state of the UK economy, still reeling from the banking crisis of 2007/8. In the midst of this the general public are informed that the provision of welfare to disabled people can no longer be afforded. Endless stories of how the country's finances are being stretched to breaking point by feckless, fraudulent claimants, then lazy working-class people and immigrants, roll off the presses; all this while a massive transfer of wealth from poor to rich is taking place. Billions of pounds, far in excess of anything lost through inappropriate welfare claims, are also being lost through tax avoidance by the rich. Understandably welfare recipients are confused by the sudden deluge of attacks upon them. The considerable numbers of the population who are turning against their fellow citizens in attack have been steered away from discerning the true nature of the conflict in their midst. Their anger and outrage are the result of mystification. The real nature of the conflict people face – an onslaught upon their living standards by the super-rich, which is part of what Jeffrey Winters (2011) has referred to as the politics of wealth defence – is thereby evaded.

When we consider the worth of alienation and mystification as explanatory concepts for elucidating the nature of social reality, as social scientists we must remain mindful of the need for reflexivity. This requires that we consider how psychological theory itself may actively participate in reproducing them. For example, the accepted paradigm within neuroscience and cognitive psychology in general is to position human beings not as active agents in shaping and determining the conditions of their existence but as complex bio-computational organisms for whom free will is an illusion. This has long been recognised in philosophical circles as a critical political and moral question. Nietzsche saw in the abolition of free will the abolition of meaning and purpose, which leads to irremediable problems not only for ideas of progress in the sciences but for the notion of scientific progress predicated upon the meaning and interpretation of evidence. At issue here is whether *we choose* to produce accounts of the human condition – and human political activity is an essential feature of it – which are of themselves alienating and which may by way of this hinder the development of alternative possibilities for envisioning constructive social change. Marx's humanist conceptual repertoire thus asks us to consider what effect our theories have on the world, as well as how well they fulfil their task of explaining it.

Psychology, Alienation, Mystification

Modern psychology, in service to the globalised ideology of capitalism, has – if anything – contributed greatly to this alienated view of ourselves. As embodied, thinking, feeling, loving, experiencing creatures imbued with a sense of self, human beings have all but disappeared from the theoretical and practical mainstream of the discipline – a shock to which every generation of psychology students has had to rapidly adjust. Eliminated from the subject matter of the behavioural sciences, the person as a centre of experience has been supplanted by the "zombie," celebrated by philosopher Dan Dennett (1992, p.405) as "behaviourally indistinguishable" from a "normal human being." This helps psychologists to evade the perennial mysteries of individuality and of consciousness – the latter said to be "materialism's biggest problem" (Sheldrake, 2012, p.109), the former scarcely recognised as a problem – and to continue the relentless celebration of the automatic. As we consume one another for the edification of the market, zombies and their vampire cousins raise their un-dead heads with disconcerting regularity – anywhere from late-night TV to the local high street – in what seems to be a suitable metaphor for how we are encouraged to relate to one another. This apocalyptic vision reduces human existence to a serial collectivity ruthlessly competing in an eternal Darwinian struggle for survival – an essentially disorganised anti-social ensemble driven to consume, devouring all comers in its wake – much like the agents behind the international financial system exposed by Bakan (2005) as corporate psychopaths.

The forms of alienation (from self, other, work and economic control) which shape the contours of our psychological reality are exacerbated by the discipline of psychology which purports to be a neutral science of mind and behaviour. Rather than contesting these forms of alienation, psychology not only exacerbates them but moves to celebrate them in a positivist "carnival of inauthenticity" (Boym, 2010, p.104). Alienation from self is actively encouraged by psycho-biological frameworks – particularly behaviour genetics and neuroscience – which permeate the discipline and challenge and undermine notions of free will, agency, responsibility and morality. Subject to the petrifying gaze of the natural sciences – a club to which psychology yearns to belong – human beings are studied as if we were nothing more than complex mechanisms, utilising a value-free approach to humanity which mirrors the value-free operations of the market and depoliticises the causes of much of our distress.

This obsession with being a natural science leads to an obsession with measurement and a rigid stance which holds that the study of anything that cannot be measured – and human subjectivity and experience of the world are prime examples of what cannot be measured – is not scientific and therefore is of less importance. What cannot be measured cannot be used, so the reasoning goes. The socially, culturally, politically, economically and historically de-contextualised human being which emerges from the centre of reductionist psychological theorising has serious consequences for how we think about the various ills (social, political, economic, cultural and psychological) that befall us and consequently how they can be addressed. Left utterly alone, it is the individual woman or man who must be held solely accountable for their fate, a stance that facilitates victim blaming: each individual becomes the source of their mental and physical problems, a desirable state of affairs for governments of a neoliberal political persuasion and for the slave-master corporations to which they bow down. As an example we have a curious branch of political psychology rooted in social cognition which seeks to locate the source of any politically undesirable or reprehensible behaviour (anti-Semitism and nationalism are two of the leading candidates) in the cognitive structures and predispositions of individuals. Somewhat akin to a search for original sin, the approach – which by nature is anti-historical – is not only guaranteed to fail miserably but in so doing to divert attention away from the organised features of the world, both enduring and novel, which shape how people think, feel and act and which promote the harming of specific groups of people for ulterior and instrumentalist ends. A further consequence of this is that we are then necessarily isolated from an appreciation of the historical nature of the human social field of which we are a part.

Our alienation from others is magnified to such an extent that even the blows inflicted on us by others are seldom recognised. Over fifty years have passed since Laing and Esterson's (1964) ground-breaking studies of family life. These suggested, to the chagrin of the medical profession, that there was perhaps no such thing as schizophrenia, that even severe psychological disturbance might be understood once something of a person's social (and historical) situation was understood. Yet despite a mountain of evidence to support the validity of this position (see Bentall,

2004) it continues to receive no mention in the majority of academic psychology textbooks – books which purport to educate us in "abnormal" psychology and "psychopathology." Not only is the family (a key institution in capitalist life) protected from scrutiny in this way by psychological and psychiatric theory, but with it, by extension, all other contemporary social institutions (for example the workplace); and there is no longer one in existence that has not been infected by capitalist logic.

The alienation promoted by theory has manifested itself in other ways too. One has been the isolation of the discipline from other social sciences – chiefly history, sociology and literature – such that activity within the discipline is increasingly impervious to the knowledge generated outside of its rigid boundaries. A similar rupture also exists between economics and ecology. To add to these intra-disciplinary ills, the imposition of market forces upon global higher education has had a catastrophic effect on critical thought in the discipline – with a form of biological fundamentalism privileged in both funding and career advancement. Consequently the divorce of the discipline from people's everyday concerns has reached unprecedented levels and this speaks of alienation not just in the Marxist sense but also of a deep alienation from worldly concerns.

The problems do not end with academic psychology producing an alienating picture of the human condition, one which is "neither appealing nor very meaningful" (Arendt, 1978, p.35). We must also consider the second component in Marx's explanation for the human propensity to surrender to subjugation – mystification. With this in mind, we can see that a good deal of psychological theory as well as being alienating is also mystifying. Conflicts between people and the everyday difficulties and stresses that people encounter (most of the psychological difficulties that people present with are actually concerned with their relationships with other people), which may

sap their energy, will, joy and desire, are theoretically recon-
figured. Thus they are not the result of ongoing or prior difficult
circumstances but defects in biochemistry or genetics at one end
or "self-efficacy" or "resilience" at the other – all characteristics
of their defective individuality. In this way the reality of our
problems in living become mystified as interiorised disease
processes. Political, social and interpersonal issues are discussed
as if they were actually medical problems – part of what psychi-
atrist Thomas Szasz (2007) referred to as the medicalisation of
everyday life. Marx's explanation for false consciousness, identification with one's oppressors and the goals they espouse
(including support for the diversionary tactics of racism, attacks
on the poor, objectification of women, defence of the status quo,
non-recognition of a fundamental class conflict) is that it is
produced by a combination of alienation and mystification. The
irony is that a good many of the people who embark on a psychological education do so with the intention of improving people's
lives. Their hopes are to effect widespread change in people's
well-being. They are misled – mystified even – into thinking that
psychology, both in its academic and psychotherapeutic guises,
offers the best way to do it. Perhaps part of the problem is that
they quickly learn not to see themselves at the centre of their
psychological mission. Having heard nothing of Marx
throughout their training, they become, like the philosophers he
criticised, only interested in interpreting the world rather than
seeking to directly intervene in it and change it.

   In examining forms of alienation and mystification we have to
not only consider how psychological theory itself may actively
participate in reproducing them – and thereby hinder the development of alternative possibilities for envisioning constructive
social change – but also draw attention to limitations inherent in
Marx's understanding of the forms of dislocation possible
between people (individuals or groups of individuals) and the
society in which they exist. Marx saw such dislocation as inher-

ently negative. However when we later come to examine Boym's (2001, 2008, 2010) theorising of the "off-modern" and her notion of estrangement *for* the world as opposed to estrangement *from* it, we will be confronted with a very different picture of the creative possibilities which may reside there, one which implicitly challenges not only Marx's view of human nature and his vision of constructive social change but also what we consider as psychological knowledge and who "owns" or commands it.

Michel Foucault

Foucault's work spans the history of ideas, the nature of historical change and the relationship between power and knowledge. Along with Marx, Freud and Darwin, he is committed to removing the individual subject from the centre stage of history. In Foucault's eyes the human tide sweeping through events is a systemic and collective wave, not an individual project. Collective authorship – if authorship can be said to exist at all – reigns at the expense of the individual control of destiny. The sea of concepts with which we exercise our understanding of reality thus functions as an anonymous ensemble, devoid of consciousness, located beyond individual reach, generating discourses of power and knowledge. These, through their own internal architecture and dynamic potential, direct the flow of human progress – if there is such a thing – shaping the practices of culture, arts and science in unpredictable but coherent ways. In *The Archaeology of Knowledge* (2002), Foucault seeks to discern the organising principles that underpin the evolution and development of discourse principally within what are currently constituted as the human sciences. Though important as social theory, he considers Marxism unsuited to this task (Gutting, 2005), though he, like Marx, embraces a dialectic in which contradiction is the engine of discursive change.

One of the specific challenges that this project poses for psychology – indeed for all branches of psychology – is that

Foucault nowhere accepts the *a priori* legitimacy of existing subject boundaries. For him such fields as "psychopathology, medicine or political economy," for example, are "dubious unities" (Foucault, 2002, p.29), useful only in so far as they may resist interrogation or alternate reformation from a field of discursive events. Likewise the objects of discourse themselves (e.g. madness, political economy, history) may have no inherent objectivity to them but be defined by a set of practices which seek to insert them as solid entities into the fields of discourse. His analysis is consequently not one which seeks to reveal "contact between a reality and a language [...] the intrication of a lexicon and an experience" (ibid, p.54).[10] Reality is thus constructed and known only through discourse. In one way or another the clashing discourses in psychology and the imprecision in delineating exactly what are the objects of study within various branches of the discipline (and this includes political psychology) calls into question not merely its future survival – in the fragmented form in which it currently exists – but also its current claim to legitimate scientific status. This status is properly seen as an assertion whose claim to truth rests on the power behind the assertion. It is of interest that social and political psychologists who have applied Foucault's insights to their own domains of operation have in general not sought to interrogate the legitimacy of that domain. Criteria of competence and knowledge to interrogate reality in a specific manner are invariably self-proclaimed and rest on an institutional authority that is anything but simple. Parker is a rare exception in this regard, seeing psychology primarily not as a natural science, but an "ideological system [...] and coercive apparatus for normalising and pathologising behaviour" (cited in Hepburn, 2003, p.47; see also Parker, 2007).

As suggested above Foucault also challenges the existing anthropological categorisation of events (e.g. intentionality, the authorship of text) and the terms we employ to denote modes of relatedness between events – whether discursive or otherwise. When Foucault questions the understanding behind such terms as "influence," "cause and effect" or "correlation" he seems to be arguing for a more fluid conception of the territory under investigation, bringing to mind the work of Kurt Lewin whose field theory is neglected and largely forgotten in social psychology. In Lewin's formulation a field denoted all modes of relatedness between individuals and their environment at a given moment of time, as well as the influence the field may have on its own subsequent development – including the actions of the various actors and objects currently and at some future point in time contained within it. Thus, in Lewin's framework a social field can be self-propagating. This has similarities with Foucault's notion of a "discursive field" which binds together language, social institutions, power and forms of subjectivity across different times and places, and which defines "the possible positions of speaking subjects" (Foucault, 2002, p.137). The connexions between events, actors and objects are thus inherently probabilistic and the expression of simple chains of cause and effect poorly suited to addressing them. Foucault's thought thereby stands apart from the mechanistic determination of history favoured by Marx and appeals to a more holistic hermeneutic framework – a temporally bound field of meaning. In this respect the discursive articles of unchallengeable common sense that populate the Foucauldian universe share something of the flavour of the common myths that inform Boym's work (see Boym, 1994 for example) and Moscovici's (2000) theory of social representations. The discipline of psychology however, while recognising the uncertainty inherent in the human arena, has clung steadfastly to a deterministic philosophy reminiscent of nineteenth-century physics – hoping to maintain its status as a science by doing so and consequently eschewing the values implicit in a discursive qualitative reckoning with human life.

Disciplinary Regulation

A Foucauldian analysis favoured by Parker (2007) sees in psychology's political and functional role a new form of disciplinary regulation – a branch of knowledge on the expanding tree of statistical science, which arose as a key moment in the evolution of surveillance. In tracing these new forms of disciplinary regulation of the human subject back through time, Foucault is following in the wake of Nietzsche's genealogical method. In drawing attention to the irruption of profoundly new historical events which instigate new networks, fields of influence and patterns of relationship into the human realm, there are interesting parallels with Arendt's ideas – though Foucault exhibits a marked disdain for abstracting, pinpointing or highlighting points of origin in a discursive field, save to say they are born of contradiction. Arendt in contrast envisages each human presence on the planet as opening up and constituting unequivocally new points of departure and freedom within the human landscape. A key difference with Foucault is that whereas Arendt is at pains to stress the "mystery of individuality," Foucault finds little interest in such a perspective. For him it is not individual human actors who are seen as exerting agency, so much as particular discursive regimes and the modes of experience available to actors within a given discursive field that constitute their subjective position. This is a theoretical position more at home with the identity politics of the twenty-first century than an avowedly existential stance embracing the rich details of lived individual experience or individual creativity. Discourse thus governs one's subjective place in the world and enfolds freedom within a set of disciplinary (in both senses of the term) practices.

Discursive Regimes, Freedom and Power

Nietzsche's "will to power" (the attempt to escape the infinite regress of cause-and-effect relationships in a deterministic world) is supplanted in Foucault's work by a "will to truth" emanating from the "agency" of particular discursive regimes. The subject then is not "free" in a sense of possessing or embodying the freedom to choose from existing alternatives or to initiate new courses of action because for Foucault there is "no privileged status for the conscious content of [...] thought" (Gutting, 2005, p.35); the thinker is proclaimed to be dead in much the same way as the author.[11] Foucault avowedly aims at nothing less than the abolition of all interiority (Foucault, 2002, p.232), a position evocative of Dennet's (1995) theoretical invocation of the human actor as zombie, and one which is problematic for the emancipatory rhetoric present in the writings of many who have followed his thought.

The problems are twofold – first of all the abolition of the thinking, feeling, experiencing subject from the genesis and maintenance of discursive regimes would appear to ignore important ethical questions. If one can properly trace the perpetration of evil – at least in part – to the power tied up with particular discursive regimes, then Foucault's analysis would seem to absolve human actors of all responsibility. The operation of power through discourse consequently would then also lack a moral foundation. A question in reading Foucault is whether morality is seen as contingent upon intentionality or as the descriptive labelling of a field of discourse. By this same token, if power is displaced into a zone of amorality, it would perforce lack any intentional emancipatory possibilities, being theoretically severed from any possible alliance with political projects instigated, organised and directed by human beings toward the *intended* realisation of their own liberation and freedom. It is of interest that when interviewed by Rabinow (1991), Foucault was adamant that power relations must perforce always involve relations of domination. In this respect his thought is discordant with strands of Eastern thought, notably associated with Buddhist practise (and at least some schools of martial arts, (e.g.

Kwit, 1981), which point to the benign use of force as a core ethical position and practical possibility. With avowed domination always a reality in the Foucauldian world, his position is consistent with a view of history as the replacement of one form of tyranny by another. A manifest weakness in Foucault's conception of power – he sees it as "only a certain type of relation between individuals" (Foucault, 1978, cited in Chomsky & Foucault, 2006, p.208) – is that it ignores the obvious and far-from-hidden realities of institutional power (political and military for example), and the inertial almost obstinate power of systems resistant to change.

Secondly if the experiential subject is irrelevant to the onward march and transformation of discourse, one wonders what the purpose of discursive regimes actually is – as opposed to their function. If human intentionality is an absence at the heart of a discursive field then that very field by definition cannot be intentionally harnessed toward a good – such as the general well-being of the individual/group or their freedom from suffering – when Foucault, on his own admission, has proposed the abolition of all interiority. Without such necessary interiority and intentionality there can be no starting point for an emancipatory discourse predicated on improving the human condition. Foucault's contribution to the history of ideas would seem to be a creation – a multiplying, metamorphosing, transforming, discursive entity which marches through time at once feeding upon and shaping the minds of its hapless human prey. The parallels with Dawkins' evolutionary memes are at once apparent.

Foucault's thought in this respect leaves no space for the human subject to be considered free – not even in the limited sense of being able to participate in the generation and maintenance of discursive regimes which might then come to enjoy a life and momentum beyond the person (or persons) – while being subject to the meanings, power and regulatory dynamics of the regime. Foucault's thesis accordingly begs the question as to how particular discursive regimes ever get started. His assertion that discourse is both "a unity and discontinuity in history itself, posing problems of its own limits" (2002, p.131) could be read as an invitation to a socio-cultural form of Arthurian mysticism – the search for the origin of discourse taking on the mantle of the search for the Holy Grail. Far more useful, plausible and tangible is Boym's (2010) idea of "co-creation" – of human social networks comprising part of the "conditions of possibility" (Foucault, 2002, p.xxii) for a given type of thought to arise at a historical moment. This would enable one to maintain human agency as a driving force behind the emergence of discursive regimes, leave a place for it at the heart of the social nexus, while still recognising the inertial power and momentum of discursive regimes. Foucault however, to repeat, sees no such place for individual human subjectivity in this – for him discursive regimes involve relations of "exteriority" which are not premised on an "unfolding manifestation of a thinking, knowing, speaking subject" (2002, p.60). It is almost as if Freud has been turned inside out – and that the structures that daily govern people's thoughts and actions, but of which they are unaware, belong not so much in the unconscious mind as the "unconscious" society, a notion that has more than a passing degree of kinship with Lacan's notion of the "Big Other." Foucault seems to have bequeathed a marriage of convenience between Lacanian psychoanalysis and Dawkins' anti-scientific sociobiological reductionism. So in Foucault, as with Marx, the relationship between the individual and the social remains deeply problematic. The question of "What matters, who is speaking?" (Foucault, cited in Rabinow, 1991, p.101), Foucault's double death sentence to the author (syntactically and figuratively), remains central therefore to delimiting not just the aesthetics and politics of the human sciences but also their purpose and integrity – in fact to the very humanity with which they speak to both the joyful and dark possibilities latent in the human condition.

Politics and Governance of the Self

Despite Foucault's elimination of the subject from the history of thought, his key works in the field of madness, sexuality and punishment have opened up emancipatory challenges to existing structures of power. It was Laing who introduced Foucault's work on madness to the English-speaking world and thereby aided his ascent to the "anti-psychiatry" pantheon. The term is of course problematic (see Szasz, 2009 for a critique) but there is little doubt that Foucault's thought emboldened many to challenge the mainstays of medical power, sexual repression and social control – all of which the modern psychiatric system functions to regulate. The histories of madness, sexuality and punishment elaborate the three genealogical axes that concern Foucault – truth, power and ethics – and create the basis for a history of the subject describing the development and confluence of political and ethical practices concerned with the governance of the self. The self – understood in social constructionist parlance as an abstraction – is nevertheless housed within the body. Hence, the various means of "self-regulation" that come to be practised involve various disciplinary activities on the body. In this "bio-political" arena the human body occupies centre stage in political struggle – which is as much a struggle with ourselves as a struggle with exterior political authority. Foucault's insight is to identify in this struggle a practice of internalising the gaze of the powerful other so that we become both the perennial guard and the perennial prisoner. Awareness of policing our thoughts and actions in order to satisfy this imagined gaze of the other, provides endless possibilities for capitalist enterprise to sell us the antidote to the manufactured and inevitably perceived gap between self and perfection. Foucault is thus rightfully wary of the endless preoccupation with sex as having much relevance for human liberation. The Western desire – indeed obsession – to free oneself from sexual hang-ups in the name of liberation is rather like an instruction not to think of pink elephants, an exercise doomed to failure as any attempt to escape from the snare simply tightens the rope. It is in the examination of the "un-freedoms" of the self that Foucault's denial of human freedom and intentionality appear most plausible. The danger in reading Foucault, however, lies in drawing pessimistic conclusions about the possibility of freedom from the contemporary historical enslavement of the self. For Foucault it would seem that individual human freedom (or its absence) is inextricably and of necessity bound up with these conditions of the self. In contrast, both Arendt and Boym would contend, based on their own experiences and analyses of life in the twin totalitarian theatres of the twentieth century, that there is an ineradicable core of freedom at the heart of the human condition, within which there lies the perennial hope of both resistance and creativity.

Svetlana Boym

The Off-Modern

Like Foucault, Boym's contribution to this debate comes from outside the discipline of psychology. Her work critically engages with the modernist project, fashioning an innovative challenge to how we "do" psychology and what we consider viable research findings. Psychology as well as its neglected cousin, psychotherapy, may be said to embrace key aspirations of the project of modernity.[12] Modernity's hijacking as a critical outlook on contemporary life means that it is now much misunderstood. Instead of this critical stance it is now misconstrued as a reference to the continual "progress" wrought by mechanisation and the drive to industrial "modernisation." This view of modernity assisted by reductionist science – with science and technology the twin pillars in the actualities of capitalist modernisation – has given us the form of psychological practice that we have today, one that is seen in some quarters as divorced from everyday concerns (Itten & Roberts, 2014). Like Kundera's (1996, p.6) despised intellectual it "does not understand life" and stands "cut off from the people," a product of modernisation, though with little to say about it.

While Fromm sees psychology as perpetuating alienation – with the discipline stranded in "a desert of organized forgetting" (Kundera, 1996, p.218), Boym seeks to reinvigorate modernity as a critical project, beginning from the very fact of dislocation and articulating the creative and human possibilities that reside in it. Eschewing the fashion for "post-"led neologisms fashioned by theorists to signal the end of modernity, she instead articulates an alternative intellectual history of modernity through her concept of the "off-modern." This, she writes, "doesn't follow the logic of crisis and progress but rather involves an exploration of the side alleys and lateral potentialities of the project of critical modernity" (Boym, 2008, p.4). In so doing, "unforeseen pasts and ventures" may be recovered. "It opens into the 'modernity of what if' rather than simply modernisation as it is" (Boym, 2010c). Boym's expansive elaborations of the off-modern reposition and reinvent the psychological within a cultural phenomenology of political and everyday history, suffused with a fragile temporality encompassing people, places, language, memory, imagination, emotion, art, artefact and home. Here we witness a seamless merging of the search for meaning, dignity, love, and freedom in individual life with a broader political canvas in which the ghosts of past actions – and inactions – inhabit the urban and domestic spaces of the real and the might-have-been.

The beauty of this exposition – a markedly different approach to the psychological and potentially the psychotherapeutic – is that, while the full richness of a psychological framework is maintained, it is not privileged. Though Boym's work is elaborated within a critical tradition of comparative literature as well as architecture and aesthetics, it embraces many disciplinary interests and invites us to rethink the purpose of psychological enquiry and practice. It becomes possible to imagine psychology (or psychologies) as less concerned with explaining the material workings of the human organism and our statistical commonalities,[13] and more with addressing how we actually deal with the complexities of being and having been in the world; a psychology imbued with an elusive and fragile sense of time passing, and of our appearance and disappearance from it – a sense felt more acutely as one ages. The question of how to deal with it is, after all, the one that generations of psychology students thought they were signing up to and were subsequently taught to forget.

Consequently an off-modern psychology brings to the social and political some of the paradoxical features of the quantum world, opening doors to "a superposition and co-existence of heterogeneous times" (Boym, 2001, p.30) questioning established narratives of "progress" and assumptions of linear social time. Boym's (2010) articulation of freedom in a co-created human world poses serious challenges to a psychology predicated on an assumed unproblematic answer to the age-old question: "What must the world be in order that we may know it?" (see Arendt, 1978, Book 2, p.199). Having defied the efforts of Hegel and Marx to impose any lawful regularity upon it, history is demonstrably neither orderly nor rule-governed. But there is also the likelihood that the world may in some fundamental way be unknowable in the present sense of what we mean by knowledge; that in our attempts to grasp and fix reality cognitively by carving it up into discrete knowable things we are doomed to failure. A good deal of European philosophy over the last century – from Bergson to Derrida – as well as Eastern philosophy over a much longer period, has made the same point in vastly different ways. How then we approach questions of being, knowing and doing when the primary ontological basis of reality is one of becoming rather than being is of vital importance for psychology. An off-modern psychology might bring to this challenge a more artistic, interpretative and performative stance, not just at ease with changing and modifying the world in an attempt to comprehend it but as a form of action that both mirrors and comprises part of the world in knowing. I am brought back to Laing and Kelly's failed attempts to establish a legitimate science of persons – one where the objectifying gaze turned us either into things or numbers. An off-modern *art of persons* offers prospects for knowledge, personhood, action, freedom and creation as it simultaneously avoids the glare of the petrifying gaze of science and precludes any necessity to confine the rhythms of momentary invention to the practice of psychotherapy. "Art into Psychology," like Vladimir Tatlin's slogan of "Art into Life," seeks to "open horizons of imagination [...] beyond mechanistic clichés" (see Boym, 2010b, p.63).

This raises further questions about the utility of, and the limits to, the distinction between procedural and declarative knowledge. It also opens up for re-evaluation the dialectic between the organic phenomenal world of experience and the quest for a form of knowledge that aims to theorise and reduce all facets of existence to the operation of immutable and timeless laws and principles – a position whose wisdom even some physicists have begun to question (see Unger & Smolin, 2015). The recognition by scientists and philosophers of a creative principle at work in nature reinforces the prerogative of art to deny its strangeness and uniqueness to the operation of fundamental causal laws. Perhaps what is needed in place of a theory of experience is a new "politics of experience" (see Itten & Roberts, 2014) combined with what Derrida referred to as a "performative commitment" to political experience (Glendinning, 2011, p.84), both of which might seek to insert questions of justice into our performative plays on knowing.

For the oldest of the sciences to embrace the reality we seek to know as one fundamentally historical in nature and in flux will have knock-on effects on how we conceptualise scientific method, in all the currently recognised natural sciences. A rapprochement between Eastern and Western philosophy is one possibility, with science making its way in a free-flowing epistemological river as but one form of art. The scientific arts would be concerned with developing understanding of the myriad forms of relationship existing between the processes, events, circumstances and forms of being (living and non-living, natural and constructed) which are seen to exist in the world. There is no reason that such understanding should elevate the role of mechanistic causes and effects above all else. The temporal relations between events, particularly in the human world, are predicated on meaning, agency, intention and contingency – all viable themes for a dissenting scientific art.

Consistent with Feyerabend's notion of methodological pluralism – that in matters of science "anything goes" – a merger between East and West might simultaneously pave the way for a philosophy of science to merge with a philosophy of the arts. As Unger and Smolin (2015) contend, science does not provide privileged knowledge over other sources of experience and insight. What distinguishes one science from another and science from art is simply the domain of reality into which they enquire and the means by which they do so.[14] Neither undertaking provides any final answers to the problems of existence, though they may certainly enrich human life. To say that both scientific and artistic products are cultural and provisional, does not mean they are arbitrary. Dali's paranoiac critical landscapes tell us something actual about the disintegration of both rationality and certainty in twentieth-century life, to say nothing of the multiple modes of consciousness opened up by psychoanalysis and LSD. Similarly the design, construction, colonisation and occupation of public space by commercial images says something tangible and real about the power of the image as well as the ownership of public space. How these modify our visions of individual and collective self-identity from the constructed past to the imagined future through the disappearing present are real enough – certainly just as real as anything bequeathed by fashion-conscious scientist photographers.

The common goals of arts and science are to articulate meanings to being in the world, their common repertoire of actions being to interrogate, challenge, represent, reproduce and reiterate reality. Both are progressive in that they build on prior research products in their field and solve problems by invention. In the different spheres of art and science the domain worlds they inhabit exhibit different degrees of stability and regularity and hence place different demands on the kinds of "results" which will prove useful to this quest. There is no intrinsic separation between art and science on the basis that the latter must involve mathematics. While mathematics has made great contributions to scientific understanding it is neither a necessary nor a sufficient condition of scientific practice. The mistaken view that it is has played a major role in distorting what economics and psychology, for example, are capable of telling us about human behaviour, inventiveness, good will, reciprocity and exchange. It is also worth remarking that mathematics itself is not what it is sometimes thought to be. Gödel's work in the first half of the twentieth century put an end to the hope that a single powerful formal axiomatic system would be capable of generating all mathematical truths. One of the consequences of this is that mathematical activity can be viewed as a creative art. Notwithstanding its successes, there is no intrinsic or necessary relationship between mathematical expression and what occurs in nature. Some aspects of reality – human consciousness being just one of one of them – may not be computable, that is, explained on the basis of any formal rule-based system.

In recent years mathematics-envy has created serious problems in many areas of science, notably where its elegance and internal coherence has become a mistaken byword for physical or psychological reality. In cosmology mathematical models of the universe have frequently been treated as if they are a form of empirical data about reality, whilst in neuroscience the complexities of the data-processing algorithms – used for example to produce magnetic resonance images of the brain – are considered as if they are providing direct access to a hidden reality.[15] Problems abound in psychology also where the outcomes of complex multivariate statistical procedures, by virtue of their complexity alone, irrespective of whether they are ever replicated (usually they are not), create the impression that some nugget of truth has been revealed. The same is true of molecular genetic research in psychiatry. What all these have in common is that mathematical and data-processing complexity are now treated as if they are a criterion of truth. While technology advances and a considered knowledge and under-standing of what these procedures are actually doing comes to be held by fewer and fewer people, the possibilities of other members of the scientific community, let alone those outside it, challenging received wisdom is correspondingly reduced. The resultant dangers are all too obvious. As Blackburn (2005) has noted, when it comes to matters of truth, justifying a view of reality is not the same thing as getting it right, and we know power casts a long shadow when it comes to self-serving justifi-cations. While it may be legitimate to treat reproducible empirical data as an extension of our senses, the process of inference is not straightforward. With the use of any tool – whether the telescope or an MRI scanner – it is imperative to convincingly demonstrate that the reality of what is being brought closer to the human eye (or the human mind) is not unjustly distorted. A critical appreciation of the context of data, of explanation, of interpretation and of action is vital. If I was to hazard a guess, I would say that the critical mind set needed for this task is increasingly absent from a science education and is more likely to be found in the arts. A marriage of the two offers the best prospects and a move back to technological minimalism in investigation, where possible, would be a helpful adjunct. The potential radical realignment of arts and sciences carries enormous implications not only with regard to how we acquire and cultivate the requisite emotional awareness and practical and intellectual skills in any one discipline, but also for how the processes of learning and developing these are facilitated, legitimated and institutionalised. It has often been said that the future is another country. Existing disciplinary boundaries seem increasingly ill-equipped for the tasks of preparing for it and living in it. Perhaps the concept of the off-modern opens up a different way of exploring and inhabiting the world.

Estrangement

Explorers in the landscape of the off-modern may be assisted in their adventures by becoming acquainted with the art of estrangement described by Soviet artist Viktor Shklovsky (2005, 2015). The Slavic roots of the word suggest both distancing and making-strange. What Shklovsky is getting at here is a radical dislocation from one's usual point of view, a reframing and re-contextualisation of reality; one moreover that affords an entirely different set of possibilities – for perception, understanding and action – which enhance one's (and others') life. From initially being an artistic technique, estrangement morphed into an existential art and practice of freedom (Boym, 2005, p.581). This is what Boym has in mind when she speaks of estrangement *for* the world – it breathes new life into the possibilities of being and resurrects the "ordinary marvellous" (ibid, p.583) under the all-encompassing challenges of life. Hence she makes profound connections with a number of authors including Arendt, Baudelaire and Benjamin. Each of these in their own way stressed the importance of renewal and new beginnings in life's affairs – pointing to the enchanting possibilities eternally present in our commonplace existence. For Arendt it was the everyday "miraculous" deed of freedom (cited in Boym, 2010, p.253), for

Baudelaire "the fantastic reality of life" (2010, p.20) and for Benjamin "the renewal of existence in a hundred unfailing ways" (1999, p.63). Boym adds her own take on "profane illumination" as moments of "time out of time" providing "re-enchantment in a minor existential key" (2008, pp.6-7). Marx's conception of alienation took in only the negative possibilities of dislocation.

That Marx missed what Shklovsky divined amidst the stultifying terror of Stalinism, is in many ways itself rather odd. It was after all Marx's own estrangement from bourgeois society that laid the grounds for him to pursue his lifelong work devoted to laying the foundations for a theoretical (and practical) understanding central to the building of what he believed would be a better society. The concepts of alienation and estrangement contain within them radically different versions of what it means to be free. Within the Marxist framework, freedom resulted from overcoming alienation, whereas Shklovsky divined estrangement as a continual possibility to work against the habitual familiarity of life. So that where Marx proposed liberation and emancipation as solutions to the enigma of being conditioned in an oppressive society, Shklovsky saw the expression of liberation and emancipation embodied in a continual "exercise of wonder, of thinking of the world as a question, not as a staging of a grand answer" (Boym, 2005, p.587).

There are many more obvious examples than Marx's theoretical struggles of how estrangement may work in a positive direction. Perhaps the most instructive of these is the story of the campaign to unseat Chilean dictator Augustus Pinochet after years of state-sponsored repression, fear, torture, sudden "disappearances" and mass murder. Told in Pablo Larrain's (2012) film *No*, the lesson was that the fear-provoking capacity of the regime was vulnerable to an assault not by arms but by art – a political art attack. The vision of an alternative future and freedom from tyranny was rendered visible through humour, music and a dramatically lived joy on the Chilean streets. The ensuing political change owed more to this than any strategic program promising an end to the regime's corruption and barbarity. In the face of the artistic and entertainment onslaught, the dread of Pinochet withered and even his own generals deserted him.

We might further argue that irony, humour and comedy are closely bound to estrangement. Estrangement for example lies at the heart not only of comedy – in which a portion of the world is first made strange (defamiliarised) and later returned (familiarised) with a punchline – but also all creative opposition and resistance to power, even overwhelming power. The Russian punk band Pussy Riot's "gig" in Moscow's largest cathedral is an interesting example, using music, performance and costume to out the relationship between the Orthodox Church and the increasingly authoritarian Russian State (see *Express Tribune*, 2012). Such action against political terror is estranging precisely because it is action in the face of the assumed impossibility of action – the seeming inevitability of fearful paralysis itself immobilised.

Art and Dissent

The work of estrangement is often directed to intentionally undermining a taken-for-granted "truth." In a reworking of Nietzsche's famed aphorism it is Batman's nemesis, the Joker (played by the actor Heath Ledger in Christopher Nolan's film *The Dark Knight*), who tells us what we have long known from experience but seldom if ever articulated: "Whatever doesn't kill you makes you stranger." This might be adapted still further to address the inherent possibility of growing from life's challenges: "Whatever doesn't kill you can be estranged!" Ledger's Joker however does not manage this – he is estranged and alienated *from* the world – even as he is playing with (and estranging) our notions (various fantasies of childhood trauma) of how he came to be so. Boym's and Shklovsky's readings of estrangement are powerful reminders that there are political options other than surrender or defeat – and that, unlike the favoured motif of dystopian science fiction, resistance is not "futile." Boym reflects "we have to do what it takes to exercise the modicum of freedom – defined by Hannah Arendt as a 'miracle of infinite improbability' – that occurs regularly in the public world" (2012, p.8).

In London, in 2015, an exhibition at the Victoria and Albert Museum entitled *Disobedient Objects* examined the use of art by political movements intent on social change. The objects on display included banners, defaced currency, textiles bearing witness to political murders, designs for barricades and blockades as well as video games and inflatable balloons bearing political messages. The objects preserved a social memory of oppression and resistance and invited public participation to engage in the construction and dissemination of an alternative knowledge of the past with an implicit message that justice can never be served without full knowledge and memory of the past. Estrangement as resistance and freedom thus is a means of rebuilding and preserving a corner of the world from the oppressive society's rewriting of reality in its name.

The mass assault on our individual sense of reality is associated with the authoritarian and totalitarian societies of the twentieth century. However, in the early years of the twenty-first century corporate hegemony has given birth to a new variant. Policed from neither the political left nor right, the new breed of authoritarianism is situated in the shifting political centre premised on the daily rewriting of memory through public relations (a neologism coined by Freud's nephew Claude Bernays to dispel the menacing perceptions that propaganda aroused), advertising, news control and surveillance. Shklovsky saw in estrangement the miraculous possibility of maintaining wonder and joy in living. This for Boym is central – indeed art is central – to a playful dissenting serious reworking of the world, one capable of producing profound knowledge of the human condition and pointing the way to a potentially very different "order of things." In the modern age faced with global retreats into fundamentalist patterns of thought, ecological and economic degradation, it is of vital importance to keep alive hope in the possibility of the renewal of our existence. "Nothing good is ever lost," and the Buddha's words that "neither fire nor wind, birth nor death, can erase our good deeds" are further reminder of this. A descent into hopelessness, however understandable, is not justifiable.

Varieties of knowledge, technique, performance and purpose can thus be fused into an "art of resistance," challenging the notion that verbal discourse is the only appropriate performative strategy through which we may reproduce and distribute psychological knowledge. Indeed, an off-modern perspective offers a very different kind of psychology, one in harmony with Arendt's assertion that "all aspects of the human condition are somehow related to politics" (1998, p.7). It is one where imagination and reality exist side by side and function together to change the world. Art functions to disrupt the automatic perception of the status quo (Smoliarova, 2006) and hence in the context of our daily political life to disrupt unthinking acceptance of the injustices that pass for common sense. A key moment in any political struggle then becomes – as Boym argues – how to move from these moments of emergent autonomy and awareness into the arena of political dialogue, to co-create, through "dissent and deliberation," a better world. Boym's emphasis is on making the world better, not perfect! The off-modern thus not only embraces a profoundly realist political philosophy, but in doing so also firmly rejects the form of politics practiced by Stalin, Hitler, Mao and Pol Pot, which contributed to the damaged twentieth century – i.e. a politics premised on the utopian, mechanical reconstruction of the social, civil and political order. Boym reminds us: the "arts of freedom are arts. There are no rules for them." In this reading art is central to politics, central to dissent and central to participation.

Re-Centring/De-Centring Psychology

Neither Marx nor Foucault have resolved the place of human relations, human agency, emotion, experience and intentionality at the core of the world. Because of this they have also failed to resolve the problem – which Laing long grappled with – of how to produce knowledge of the human condition in a manner that accorded dignity, agency and worth to our experience of being in the world. In the broad sweeping accounts of historical process and biological destiny that underpin much of the official psychological cannon there seems no purposeful place for the variant modes, temporalities and localities of experience and action that inhabit different times and places. Scientific psychology thus remains utopian – enacting a "charismatic concealment" (Boym, 2001, p.99) of the wider horizons of psychological reality and the birth of ideas and social change. For psychology to go any way toward this it must perforce address, amongst other things, the precise (relational) content of human life as it is experienced – which as Buddhists have noticed involves a good deal of pain and suffering as well as earthly delights. Whether such a re-centring (or de-centring) of psychological knowledge, unshackled from formal professional methodology and theory, is possible is a question for all of us to ponder. It is most definitely a political question. To understand politics is not merely to create narratives of victory and defeat or of the unjust excesses of power. It is always a profoundly human challenge. In this we are required to evaluate the world through our own moral compass. This is at its most dignified where it involves "giving imaginary space to the defeated, to their impossible human choices, leaving space and acknowledging the dreams of exit in a no-exit situation" (Boym, 2010, p.275). The Archimedean point-of-view/view-from-nowhere is consequently of little use here. Given this most human requirement, an off-modern perspective warrants further consideration as the basis for a very different kind of psychology, one where dreams and reality exist side by side.

You must celebrate the morning in your blood,
For nothing dies there, nothing ends,
Over and over again you must invent yourselves,
True magicians, riding the senses of dust,
Know that with this gift you're blest
– Brian Patten (2007, p.87)

Not a whisper, not a thought,
Not a kiss nor look be lost
– W.H. Auden (1991, p.157)[16]

Three

Toward an Off-Modern Psychology

The fantasies of the past determined by the needs of the present have a direct impact on the realities of the future
– Svetlana Boym (2012, p.13)

I can't construct a stable, linear view of history
– R.D. Laing (cited in Kirsner, 2015, p.151)

Honouring the paths taken by fellow deviant travellers in the past is an important part of recovering an alternative psychology. Both Fromm and Laing, whose ideas we discussed in the previous chapter, provide us with viable examples of a form of "political" psychology that might have been. Their contributions were left by the wayside, not because of any intellectual deficiencies but because they asked undesired questions about the conventional etiquette of fantasised neutrality and human engineering. They are in a sense phantasmagorias – existing in the shadowlands between the not-quite-remembered and the not-wholly-forgotten. Laing, for his sins, estranged both the family and madness from accepted sensibilities; Fromm did the same for love. Neither, it would appear, has been forgiven. George Kelly, whose personal construct theory (1955, 1977) for a time threatened to shake up psychology, belongs in this same off-modern space.

Kelly's (1955) theory was an explicit metapsychology of the person, an attempt to get to grips with our understanding of our own understanding – the unknown world made sense of by anticipating what could be recurrently distinguished within it. Kelly was adamant that all psychological theories implicitly embrace a set of values. His approach was both existential and constructivist; all knowledge coming to us through our experience of living in a world made by us – the "architect(s)" of our "own hazards and catastrophes" (1977, p.11). I remember when I first encountered construct theory it was a refreshing flesh-and-blood change to the person-free zones offered by behaviourism and cognitive psychology. A clear theoretical advance on anything that had gone before in terms of its coherence, axiomatic structure and conceptual rigour, its failure to move centre stage within the academic world not only tells us something about the nature of progress (or the lack of it) in psychology, but also raises important questions about what psychology as a discipline is hoping to achieve – in terms of knowledge acquired, as opposed to widespread social status.

Construct theory wears its humanity on its sleeve, but that was never sufficient to rescue it from its difficulties. Trapped in American pragmatism and subject to the constraints of ideological individualism, Kelly was prevented from seeing that the acts and arts of making the world are as much a collective civic-political undertaking as an individual existential-phenomenological one. That we function well collectively to any degree depends on a consensual temporal, spatial and semantic ordering of the world. The question as to who built the material world as opposed to the experiential one was always outside the range of convenience of the framework he put forward. Consequently, Kelly and the leading construct theorists who followed in his wake never got to grips with the material questions of power and influence that shape not only the world but the psychological discourse and knowledge that is produced in it, and to which Foucault devoted some attention. The logic of "co-creation," championed by Boym and central to understanding the social foundations of the human world, mirrored by developments within sociology concerning the social production of knowledge, were simply not considered by construct theorists, who, like numerous behavioural scientists and psychotherapists, have given us an account of human life that exhibits what Brent Potter (2015, p.147) has referred to as a profound "contempt for social reality."

The "need to change" – the title of a book by Kelly's disciple, Fay Fransella (1975), was a humanistic homage to the individual struggling with his or her problematic life. What had caused or promoted the major aspects of that struggle simply could not be addressed unless they could be sourced within the framework of a person's dysfunctional construct system. The individual in crisis was thereby invariably seen as an actual or potential prisoner of their own "failed" construct system, but never a prisoner of a constructed social world which had failed human beings and which de facto set the horizon on their and others' choices. Because of its dogmatic insistence that psychology's practical focus is on individual growth and is concerned only with what goes on "inside" the mind, construct theory remained mired in an unproductive apolitical and anti-political space unsustained by any theoretical alliance it might have been able to forge across the social sciences. Berger and Luckmann's (1967) treatise on the social and interpersonal foundations of knowledge – their work marked the first time in which the term "social construction" had been employed – was more than capable of building bridges into neighbouring disciplines and eroding the increasingly problematic disciplinary boundaries. Unfortunately, because they positioned their attempt to ground common-sense consensual reality in a purely sociological paradigm, it was destined to languish on the fringes of psychological enquiry.

The chief cause of this problem was that construct theorists held many of the same presuppositions about what their scientific aims were as the assortment of colleagues distributed throughout the fragmented discipline they critiqued. Chief among these was that the focus of psychology was not in fact to explain human behaviour and meaning but to provide *psychological* explanations of these. Lacking both a clear analysis of the meaning of this distinction and a political analysis of psychology's functional role in the world at large, construct theory's radical prospectus was isolated. Butt's (2008) sympathetic appraisal of Kelly likewise misses the opportunity to connect Kelly's brand of constructivism with that which now pervades the social sciences. The problems of choice and the human-made world remain tied steadfastly to an exclusively psychological interpretation. Kelly's (1977, p.19) invitation for "getting along with the unknown," though it exhorted readers to "abandon" their "favourite psychologisms" as they reconstrued life, could not imagine the process of reconstruction extending beyond the frontiers of the individual mind.

Fransella correctly foresaw psychology as condemned to perpetual internal division unless it could come up with a coherent rationale for how and why it was studying the human subject, but because the critique she, along with Kelly and Bannister, endorsed was not interdisciplinary it was effectively adrift in an open sea, and heading nowhere, its radical prospectus soon to be exhausted. In its death throes the marketing of the theory resembled what one colleague described in the early 1980s as a construct supermarket. Marginalised from mainstream psychology from the outset, and forced to sell itself in order to survive in the burgeoning academic marketplace of the 1980s, the writing was on the wall. At the time of its effective demise, marketing and business professionals had moved in for a feeding frenzy on its empirical base and applied potential, a process that was to intensify in the 1990s and beyond.

Construct theory for all its sins was reticent to endorse the possibilities of value-free knowledge. The "view from nowhere" that is so problematic in the social sciences shines out of most publications laying claim to its theoretical foundations. Such an impossible view can never embrace what Arendt described as "the miracle of individuality," for the view from nowhere creates only objects in an eternal inert and uncreative space-time devoid of any ultimate sanctioned meaning. Though Kelly sought to honour personal uniqueness and, like Marx, envisaged human nature as an evolving expression of human "being," our actions in the world a form of asking questions of it, this was at a cost of sacrificing due respect for the materiality of existence and the world beyond the person, within which, and through which, our lives unfold. Without these important elements the fluid and poetic nature of life itself remains beyond the reach of conveniently packaged items of truth or personal constructs.

Kelly's ideas remain an oddity amongst the spectrum of ideas to have come out of psychology. Never discredited, their inability to make common cause with what permeated the rest of the discipline is crucial to understanding their failure. One unexplored response might have been to seek common cause with systems of thought that lay outside it – for the personal to engage with the transpersonal and the supra-personal – from Buddhism on the one hand to Marx on the other. As a young doctoral student I attended a conference in Personal Construct Psychology at the University of Manchester in the late summer of 1980. It was an intellectually exciting occasion with many willing to take Kelly at face value and interrogate what they saw as the limitations to the theory. I recall two specific challenges, proposed as additions to Kelly's fundamental postulate and the eleven corollaries, which are still relevant. The first of these concerned the origin of construing – how precisely was a personal construct system able to "boot itself up" from nothing? Was there a primitive core "system of origin" containing an initial set of constructs primed to do the necessary bootstrapping essential for future growth and development? This is another way of shining light into questions of human nature and whether it will ever be possible to describe, in human terms, what an "operating system" of the human organism at the default level is primed to do. Intensely psychological though the above challenge can be considered, it is not entirely separable from the second. This looked at the origin of constructs too, though from quite a different perspective, one that nowadays would sit more comfortably with social representations theory as well as work on social and collective memory. As we come into a world brimming with constructs – those of language being the obvious example – there really was a need to consider the relationship between this personal, individualised set of constructs which each person "possessed" and the social environment of constructs within which it was developing. A few of us thought that personal construct theory should be reconsidered as a special limiting condition of a broader more encompassing framework – we brazenly suggested this could be called something along the lines of "social construct theory" – which would carry the weight of the collective and historical dimensions of meaning created in the human world and to which we were all the heirs.

Kelly's work was far from philosophically naïve and was capable of transformation and elaboration but, hemmed in by the methodological fetishism and endless desire to wall off psychology as a distinct speciality, neither of the above challenges was able to get very far. Those at the helm, who no doubt already considered their hopes of a mainstream takeover difficult enough, were not prepared to countenance what they considered acts of theoretical treachery. There are matters of pedagogy at stake here – how can a theory be taught if it is continually under change? But the subject matter of Kelly's work is not just the person. It is rather how the person changes, or fails to change, as the world around them does so. Had the opportunity been taken to adapt the theory in the above or similar ways, an additional dimension of reflexivity – itself a crucial aspect of Kelly's intentions for a humanly produced psychological theory – would have been woven into the theory's colourful cloth. Deprived of further vitality, the epistemological implications of construct theory and the ontological issues it implicitly contained thus remained insufficiently elaborated, with the outcome being, yet again, adherence to a doctrinal approach – in this case a kind of construct fundamentalism – that proved to be its own undoing.

Besides these questions of ontology, Kelly's psychological theory, with its depiction of construct systems perpetually in transition, asks questions about what we mean by truth. Again, in doing so, it stands on the margins of the discipline because of its implicit conjecture that there are no final truths to be had – no final theories are possible of what it is to be human. Kelly argued we live perennially on a horizon of knowing and becoming, alluding to a view of reality that has more in common with Lao Tzu than Skinner, Pavlov, Freud or any other of the psychological luminaries. He hints that a psychological theory has to be at ease with the nature of the world we live in – and for that to be the case we need a theory not just of the person but of the world.

The reflexive nature of construct theory ought then to have made the distinction between the knowability of the human world – that is the extent[17] to which people and the world can be known (epistemologically speaking) – and the knowability and hence feasibility of what to do in it. Kelly perhaps failed to go in this direction because he saw action as a form of construing, subject to the same strictures as cognition. Though action may legitimately be considered a form of construing, the representation of the world – whether our own personal epistemology or something collectively agreed upon – is not the same as the acts we perform in it, although it may be derived from them to a significant extent.

Representation and action are very different creatures. The former, when conscious, supplies the basis for a knowledge of the human which would facilitate (from both an external and internal perspective) prediction and control; the latter, one of how to facilitate (from the point of view of actors) not just human agency for the good of the one or the many but a direct physical change in the world. The development of our own representations can be considered a concealed change in the world not inherently or necessarily noticeable by others, while action constitutes an observable change in the state of the world. The distinction between declarative and procedural knowledge is relevant but not always watertight. We envisage action – the movement of the body through space and time – as simultaneously embodying, reflecting and creating knowledge. But it is also more than this and thereby not synonymous with representation.

Action is always in part "a leap in the dark," a means of confronting the unknown, rather than the known, its consequences always uncertain. Existing representations, for their part, are always ways of knowing and conceptualising the world, embodying a form of faith and certainty in the nature of what's out there. Action on the other hand may be a means of radically doubting it. Kelly envisaged human beings as scientists engaged in a lifelong endeavour to build a better working model of the world. From that perspective, representations can be considered the hypotheses, actions the experimental means to put them to the test. These two distinct avenues to the pursuit of science pose different and opposed political and moral questions. Representations and models of human action in the larger public sphere are unavoidably connected to the allure of prediction and control, activities which in themselves are fundamentally adversarial to aspirations of human freedom and dignity. Any form of psychology predicated on this triumvirate of prediction/control, value-free knowledge and the view from nowhere, must of necessity therefore assume that the political system within which it functions is one that is essentially benign, otherwise it must recognise its dangerous role within it. Representations, however, may exist not only consciously and publicly but unconsciously and privately. Here they are more closely allied to action. Unconscious schemas, whatever Lacan said, may exist beyond linguistic-verbal modes of apprehension and reasoning and be "storehouses" of past and potentially future actions, the basis for the forms of effortless action (see Slingerland, 2003, 2014) embodied and cultured in various schools of martial arts. Instruction and practice of these arts are intended to provide lessons for living much more than they are designed to be mere forms of physical combat.

Kelly recognised that these were important issues for a psychological theory to address. As stated he explicitly saw psychology as a set of values in action, but the collective expression in the public/political sphere of whatever these values were could not be formulated within his own framework. Thus there remains the question of to what extent his insistence on the primacy of agency and ethics can be squared both with an expressly scientific analysis (and technology) of human conduct and the wider dialectic of individual versus collective freedom.

Construct theory was criticised for being too cognitive – precisely the feature that the business fraternity found so appealing in it. This was not Kelly's intention – he stressed action in the world and our emotional grasp of it as forms of construing – but positioned within an academic regime which privileged verbal intellectual knowledge and a commitment to a scientific rather than an artistic perspective on life, the performative and poetic elaboration/exploration of its possibilities never took off. What is needed instead, if we are to avoid the contribution of psychological knowledge to alienation and potential disempowerment, is a form of knowledge that is first of all empathic and more than a little sympathetic to those it addresses – that is, explicitly biased towards those with whom it makes common cause. Bias in and of itself must be seen in the human sciences, not as an impediment to knowledge, but as an indispensable ethical ally of it (see Žižek, 2010). Our humanly produced theories about human beings cannot settle for being what Moscovici hoped his social representations theory might be, "at its best" (2000, p.280) – a "metatheory" which purports to stand above and beyond the world.

Psychological knowledge at its heart could instead seek to commemorate and celebrate the human striving to live well – or even to live at all – and to aid this and participate in an aesthetic[18] devoted to improving and renewing our lot – individually and collectively. Boym's vision reminds us that at the heart of the real world we inhabit lies the virtual world of past and future possibilities: "The fantasies of the past determined by the needs of the present have a direct impact on the realities of the future" (Boym, 2012, p.13). This means the virtual, the imaginative and the counterfactual must be grasped as central features of reality – much as they are in quantum mechanics. If a radical reworking of a viable psychology rooted in everyday life and the wonder of our earthly existence is to be possible, then to achieve it, we must radically estrange it, uproot it from its naively realist, corporate scientific soil, and get to work removing the years of overgrown weeds which have covered it. Continuing with horticultural and botanical metaphors for the moment, this will require us to step "off" the narrow and well-worn tracks of experimental psychology, invigorated with an eagerness and readiness to explore the wild undergrowth of ideas in the neglected gardens of knowledge. Abandoning a singular overarching (reductionist and utopian) narrative may be no great loss on this journey. There may be more treasures to be found in the overlooked ruins than the imagined shining palaces ahead. Instead of absorbing the regular diet of imminent scientific breakthroughs and the prescribed certainties of future success, our option is to entertain multiple partial narratives and "performative" reconstructions of self and/in the world, premised on the idea that the reality we experience is beyond lived comprehension as a singular totality and that there are ways to deal with it, interrogate it, bring it into being and know it that don't necessarily involve spoken or written language or the legitimising cloak of science. Psychology must return to being an art.

The challenge which psychologists face today in the wake of the neoliberal juggernaut's assault on the production of knowledge is not new. Shklovsky, writing in the 1920s, remarked that the Soviet artist of the day had but two choices: "to write for the desk drawer or to write on state demand" (cited in Boym, 2008, p.20). Despite the absence of a third alternative, Shklovsky argued that that was "precisely the one that must be chosen" (ibid, pp.20-1). We can take this to heart and embrace its apparent defiance of logic only if we are prepared to abandon two sacred notions.[19] Firstly, that psychology in general and political psychology in particular must eschew political statements about their own relation to the production of psychological knowledge. This would entail the "risk" of becoming, what it supposedly is in name, but evidently isn't in practice, i.e. an avowedly *political* psychology. Secondly, we must reject an epistemology of psychological knowledge that is not rooted in the everyday, in the world of people's experience of the world – of themselves, others and the material landscape which we both move through and continually create. Moscovici's theory of social representations, although it sought to remake social psychology as a "social psychology of knowledge" (2000, p.280) – a psychology of common sense as it were – has not laid bare the cultural myths that underpin the shared social consensus that props up late-capitalist societies. By positing social representations as the "principle organising agents for individual thought" (Hewstone et al., 1996, p.120) Moscovici provided the means to venture beyond the confines of individual minds while connecting the personal to the social. Despite this, its radical potential has also remained unfulfilled. Moscovici (2000, p.119) thought that social psychology had to become "dangerous" in order to be a viable critical account of everyday life.

Social representations theory, however, has become anything but dangerous. It has failed to lay bare the capitalist cultural myths, because it has remained tied to fetishised professional discursive regimes. These dictate how psychology is "performed" and stipulate its adherence to officially sanctioned methods – and publication outlets utilising "quantitative" or "qualitative" "techniques" – in order to articulate a vision *of* the world based on professional truth and not one *for* the world based on people's experience of oppression, injustice and dislocation within it. Its objects of scrutiny have come to be the circulating phantasmagorical representations themselves and not the varieties of human relationship possible and actual in the world that social representations in part mediate. Our relationships in the world are also mediated by the sheer physicality of the objects in the world – both the natural and human-made world – though in the present epoch the distinction between them, as Arendt (1998) noted, is largely superfluous. The dislocation of social representations theory from the lives of the common people whose sense and reality it aims to grasp, has more than a little to do with the values that pervade official academic disciplines and the relations between those disciplines and broader systems of power and privilege (see Giroux, 2014). That is, it raises questions about the function and purpose of professional knowledge and the systems that contain it. Social representations theory has failed, not because it does not re-present common sense but because it does not represent the voice of common sense against the tyranny that assails it. The contents of knowledge in any epistemological system always exist as relational objects to the systems of power prevailing in the world in which they are manifest.

Consequently we must articulate an epistemology of psychological knowledge that is rooted in the everyday, in the world of people's experience of the world – of themselves, others and the material (and political) landscape which we move through and continually create. In an off-modern psychology, knowledge might come from the ground up rather than the top-down variety favoured in the academy. It might be generated and discoverable in the idiopathic and idiosyncratic strategies and programs of the individuals making their way in a world existing beyond them, existing in relation to them and waiting to be discovered by them. Psychology in the off-modern vernacular could become a self-designed unlimited "course" to make sense of each person's being in the world – a journey at once critical, intellectual, artistic and practical through the multiple contextually bound complexities of reality. It is hard to countenance this as an officially sanctioned institutional discipline with its own rules, regulations and hungers for corporate funding, intellectual obedience and state approval. This "off-road" alternative is psychology as a collective project, more akin to a form of protest and discovery decoupled from the formal professional world but pursued with an intent and a purpose that is not manifest in the instrumental and "rational" modes of thought which are traditionally promoted in the academy.

Shklovsky posited the knight's move in a game of chess as the metaphorical third way when faced with a repressive binary choice. It is a three-dimensional leap in a two-dimensional space – a lateral move for creating new beginnings and asserting freedom in the face of its apparent impossibility. In the "psy-" professions one must contend with the pathologising of this manoeuvre together with the simultaneous suppression of emotion. In psychiatric parlance "knight's move thinking" is held up as prima facie evidence of a supposed "schizophrenic thought disorder" – said to be a dangerous loosening of thought away from established and accepted patterns of Aristotelian logic (Winokur & Clayton, 1994). This is but one way by which psychiatric theory and practice has violently and conceptually dislocated us from both human agency and feeling. In the case of feelings these are prone to labelling as "inappropriate affect" – emotional expression or its lack, deemed by the relevant arbiters of emotional expression to be inappropriate for a given situation – and held up as a further indication of "schizophrenic degeneration."

"Schizophrenia" is a political diagnosis wherever it occurs – always an expression of power and never one of dispassionate scientific observation. Its own fictional and mythological status is a subject all by itself. The most common diagnosis dispensed by Soviet psychiatrists upon the unfortunate "deviants" and dissidents sent packing to the gulag was "sluggish schizophrenia." This tells us something about the function of psychiatry in any repressive system and what the arts and politics of survival must contend with. However there is perhaps something further to learn here. Shklovsky's stratagem was invented in the face of a pervasive, repressive, censoring, intrusive state apparatus which functioned in such a manner that what was officially true and what was not, was difficult if not impossible to discern – a description increasingly applicable to contemporary life in the authoritarian, purportedly post-modern global city. In the face of this, many denounced themselves, believing this offered the best hope for redemption or at least freedom from torture or threats to their family. Others chose silence or resigned themselves to expulsion. This does raise the question as to whether the distress shown by those today unfortunate enough to be on the receiving end of a diagnosis of "thought disorder" is a manifestation of life within a (macro or micro) social system where open honest communication is not only in retreat but subject to a plethora of threats and sanctions, overt but disavowed, concealed and denied.

Joseph Heller's *Catch 22*, published in 1961 in the second decade of the Cold War, played a pivotal role in calling out the institutional politico-logic of the age, arguably of the century. Heller's observations and insights into the knotted human consequences of bureaucratic lunacy ran hand-in-hand with Laing's and together comprise a modern update on Kafka. Heller once asked the question which summed up years of Laing's research "What does a sane man do in an insane society?" In truth,

Shklovsky was there before them and offering an answer worthy of a Zen master. Insights into the human condition however have rarely journeyed from literature into the heartlands of psychiatry to render meaningful the plight and cries of the troubled and the wronged. Laing however joined Heller in another way: both reworked Shakespeare's musings on destiny from *Twelfth Night* ("Some are born great, some achieve greatness, and some have greatness thrust upon 'em") into their own chosen realms. Heller substituted "mediocrity" for greatness, Laing "schizophrenia." But whether it is greatness, mediocrity or schizophrenia, our fate remains as much the result of a social project as an individual one, its path never linear, and its predictability never guaranteed. Heller and Laing added to this view, a withering condemnation of the enforced structured prohibition on speaking openly about the forces that govern our fate.

The possibility of admitting this in the "democratic" West is far from easy. One need only tune in to a diet of Prime Minister's Questions in the British Parliament to see how far removed we are from a celebration of authentic and transparent communication, but as democracy withers, state brutality beckons, and lies, propaganda and misinformation saturate the official channels of communication between the 1% and the 99%. Interestingly Shklovsky also turned to Shakespeare in an ironic aside to madness and the knight's move in his essay "Apropos of King Lear." "It would be interesting to find out what disease the knight has," he wrote, "you see, he always moves in an L-shaped manner" (2005, p.94). Shklovsky's purpose in this aside is twofold: to draw attention to the constraints placed on the actor's movements, and the actor's choice in response to that – a limited act of freedom. In the theatre, as in life, one never steps into the same river twice. Lear is not internally driven but driven by circumstance – in Shklovsky's view the circumstance of the play. Of course in a game of chess the knight only moves when selected to do so; in life one may choose not to move – an option which if exercised will likely encounter a future diagnosis of catatonic schizophrenia. Shklovsky saw in Lear's madness a literary convention – and alluded to the medico-psychiatric one underpinning attributions of illness and madness. Both of these conventions blind us, the audience, to the relevant situational constraints and devices restricting liberty.

What we have been considering here in many ways are the constraints on psychology – caught in a three-way trap, seemingly locked in a netherworld by the mechanistic illusions of science, the global strictures of the market and formal multi-institutional demands which bind the practice, promotion and pursuit of a socially recognised academic subject. The question of what kind of psychology is possible in this can only be answered by a knight's move. The knight is the rebel on the chessboard; eschewing the linear, it is the only piece that may advance by going backwards. Its example opens possibilities for alternative, inherently political and avowedly humanistic paths – that is, an off-modern approach to being human. It is time to explore this more fully.

A body is given to me – what shall I do with it,
so singular and so much mine?
For the quiet joy of breathing and living
tell me, who have I to thank?
– Osip Mandelstam (1991, p.4)

Time & {Place}

Where is it that we find ourselves?
Why *are* politicians so cruel?

There are only seconds to go...

Four

Psychology of the Off-Modern: Psychogeography

We haven't really discovered how to go on talking and practicing what's called psychology, even defining it... Our epistemological insecurity is fundamental. That is we don't really know what we're doing. If that's the case then we have to articulate another... I think we have to find other forms...
– James Hillman (in Hillman & Shamdasani, 2013, p.14)

Resistance is the secret of joy
– Alice Walker (cited in Solnit, 2014, p.230)

The Psychogeographical Landscape: Paths and Moorings

Honouring the paths taken by past travellers, of revisiting the discipline's apparent "ruins" or those seemingly "ruined," is an important part of renovating psychology, of discovering, as Hillman says, how to do it. The off-modern, though it expands the realm of phenomenology, is not a purely existential pursuit, concerning as it does an assortment of unofficial shared frame-works for comprehending human existence; but neither does it oppose one. Neither are we talking about explaining "time, love and death" (Greenwood, 1999), though we may be at least permitted to recognise and consider these as fundamental features of our existence and embrace them alongside what Arundhati Roy refers to as the "God of small things." That is, we can acknowledge that the ultimate truths of our lives may be found not in grand theories but in commonplace adventure or the wondrous everyday actualised in moments of "time out of time" (Boym, 2008, p.7). Herein, the secret of joy and the truth of "the unwritten laws of everyday existence," the universal themes of life, are no secret at all – revealing themselves to unfolding experience. Lived, they can never be faithfully translated to the written word without loss.

Similarly might the off-modern evade the collective myths perpetuated by great psychologists – Pavlov, Skinner, Piaget, Eysenck and, of late, Kahneman spring to mind – who have dragged the discipline from its pre-scientific moorings into the declared open and beatific ocean of scientific truth. The truths are presumed to be universal and hence unrelated to the conditions of life of the protagonists – an assumption which, since the highpoint of Romanticism, has been somewhat more contro-versial when it comes to the appraisal of great works of art.

The furore over the supposed "death of the author" illustrates the different attitudes underlying the arts and the sciences. In common-sense perspectives, artists' works are imbued with the stamp of their personality. For scientists however their own characters are considered largely irrelevant, save perhaps their imagined genius (or should that be cultured brutality?) at prising nature's secrets from her. The concept of eccentricity, at least in the British context, is however routinely applied to the public figures of each – a vestige perhaps of society's general appre-hension about creative thinking in any genre, although there are important differences between the famed two cultures of C.P. Snow. Art, particularly modern art, is often seen as lying beyond the bounds of reason, while science, for most ordinary mortals at least, supposedly lies beyond one's reasoning capabilities, a subtle but important difference. That the heart too may be said to have its reasons has unfortunately not led to a sustained interrogation of what exactly we mean by reason in the modern context, nor what is specifically human about what its actions comprise.

Kant exhibited a keen interest in the matter – but to assume that reason in the eighteenth century is of the same process and order as reason in the twenty-first would be akin to putting the philosophical cart before the horse. Notions of reason and madness are bound to cultural times and places and should perhaps not be understood as *a priori* universal categories. Feyerabend in his dissection of the vagaries of scientific method appears to have gone some way to appreciate this – but Feyerabend aside, few have been prepared to question reason's pre-eminence or its relationship to the wider conditions of life. The seemingly inexhaustible interest in the supposed relationship between creativity[20] and madness, on the other hand, not only reflects a discomfort with innovative thought – seen as something other than reason – but also testifies to a fondness to see in certain kinds of artistic endeavour, formal aspects of character. Character above and beyond the mainstream is always, in this type of discourse, presumed to be a product of hidden genetic variables rather than the infinitely more complex hidden "work" of social, economic and cultural history or even mental history.

Our desire to fathom human history from reasoned human motives is a long one. Hegel's historical dialectic can itself be seen as an attempt to project the free human capacity for reason onto a cosmological spirit whose necessary development underscores the successive dramatic fortunes appearing on the world stage. Only the eruption of the death camp and the gulag in the twentieth century seems to have shaken our faith in the reasonableness of history or the possibility of a psychological authorship to it. Writing in the aftershock of that emergence of "subterranean" humanity, Arendt (1976, p.ix) was convinced that the dark truths of the regimes of Hitler and Stalin laid bare our inability to deduce absolute evil from comprehensible human motives, but her thought is premised on a purely psychological genealogy to reason, a view of reason and thought contained within a corporeally bounded psyche.

In the task of estranging psychology we must perforce estrange reason with it – remove it from its presumed locus within the cranium and look further afield. The mercurial city streets and parks, memory lanes or rural by-ways, in which the lives of the "great," the "terrible" and the "humble" – as well as the above roll call of psychology's finest[21] – unfold, and in which they fashioned their ideas of human nature, have been altogether unconsidered. This is both from the vantage point of any architecturally engendered psychology, by which I mean the view of the world and the possibilities within it which the structure and shape of the inhabited landscape invites, and from the perspective of the human quality and flavour of that landscape. I am speaking of the landscape of social relationships and identities which towns and cities in their amalgam of private and public spaces foster, disrupt, nurture and contain. The localities of time and place seem to have no purposeful position in the utopian vision of scientific psychology – so that what remains is a "charismatic concealment" (Boym, 2001, p.99) of the wider horizons of psychological reality and the birth of psychological ideas, nowhere more present than in the staid teaching of statistics. The science which at its inception was called "political arithmetic" ends up with the erasure of history and politics and the timeless worship of numbers.

Terrance Davies' (2008) homage to the changing face of Liverpool in the twentieth century – *Time and the City* – is a cinematic meditation on memory, reflection, time and loss, charting the changing face and culture of its people in tandem with the shifting skylines, fashions, reconstruction and destruction of its urban spaces. Davies' analysis is an alternative take on collective psychology and a starting point for imagining psychology in a different vein. That the large scale of destruction was not solely down to the Luftwaffe, but owed much to the city council's bulldozing of established communities in the name of planning, together with the ensuing wanton vandalism of dislocated and displaced young people, only adds to the bittersweet irony of it. Davies makes it easy to see how the multifaceted physical nature of the city, its history, politics, pains and pleasures, are etched into the character, creativity, resilience and submission of its inhabitants.

In my lifetime Liverpool has been rebuilt three times – structurally in the 1950s following the Blitz, culturally in the 1960s by The Beatles and the poetic avant-garde of the city,[22] and most recently regenerated after Margaret Thatcher's assault in the 1980s. The reconstructed city centre, unrecognisable from my youth, pays homage to Thatcher's worship of money and is now an architectural song of praise to conspicuous consumption. Somewhat more familiar, the crown jewels of the city, the majestic Pier Head and its beatified river environs, now resemble a gigantic outdoor art installation reimagining the maritime history which underlay the city's ascendancy to slave-trade infamy, economic prosperity and occasional inspiration for the fab four.[23] It celebrates the city in an off-modern edge, paying dual homage to economics and the counter-culture rejection of it, and with this retains that sense of the surreal that for me has always characterised life there.

Jung described Liverpool as the "pool of life." Allen Ginsberg, the Beat poet and counter-cultural icon, went one further, declaring in May 1965 that the city was "at the present moment, the centre of consciousness of the human universe." Ginsberg's eulogy also took in the local weather: Liverpool was "like San Francisco except... greyer." Living there we believed, for a while at least, that we were at the centre of the world – or at least that here was everywhere. We believed that no matter where people lived they ate never-ending quantities of fish and chips, loved football, dreamed of the future and lived in fear of unpredictable violence. By the time I left I had known four murderers – one of them being my former metalwork teacher. Another one – a local soldier – kicked me unconscious when I was about eleven. Another had head-butted me outside my friend's house – for looking or not looking at him, I was never sure. I escaped unmolested from the fourth who came into school one day to beat up the deputy headmaster. This co-existed with The Beatles singing "All you need is love." Being utterly perplexed – particular by the violence and the mass synchronous behaviour exhibited at football matches – I was led to psychology to try and fathom the human condition, for some assurance that individual existence apart from the herd mattered and that the stranger-than-fiction reality that I was embedded in could be compre-hended. The psychology I found seemed to speak to another world, a fictitious, decontextualised, cold and emotionless one where people and places, and the joys and sorrows of the inestimably large and small in life, didn't matter. Surrealism seemed a better bet and the magical realism of Latin American fiction its natural ally.

From a personal point of view, Davies' film was also thera-peutic – cinema vérité as cinema therapy. Friends who watched the film with me were visibly shocked at the level of urban decay and vandalism shown in parts, while the images of destroyed council houses – reminiscent to me of Beirut at its worst, adorned with masses of looping and colourful graffiti[24] scribbled by lost people I had once been at school with – provoked in me the type of laughter that oscillates between the painful and the pleasurable. The air we breathed was desperation itself and choked the lungs of everyone I knew. I could never have hoped to adequately describe this nor its effect. The association between the "affective geography of the land" (Boym, 2001, p.12) however and the landscape of the psyche can, as Boym notes, be traced back to the romantics, and in contemporary times "the topography of the city" is unavoidably and "intimately linked" to biography (ibid, p.134). Yet psychology scorns biography and in its stead insists that personality (a strange and abrupt condensation of invariant responses to the vicissitudes of life) and character are written in the genes, not carved into the spaces, the invisible bonds, between people and place – this despite the overwhelming evidence from life that geography, whether urban or rural, moulds people in specific ways which differ from place to place and from time to time.

In a brief review of his own family history, the economist Paul Mason (2015) takes it as given that prior to deindustrialisation the physical geography of the urban working-class cities of Northern England and the ways of life which took root there were inseparably part of the class consciousness that developed, a consciousness whose longevity was linked to the survival of the surrounds. Nobody can be known to any palpable degree without an appreciation of where in the world they are from, where they have been and where they are now. Institutional psychology is an impoverished and manifestly inaccurate account of who we are and what makes us who we are, to say nothing of who we may become. The social, economic, geographical and international climate, local history and beyond; all are layered into the structure of the psyche.

Finding parallels between urban and psychic structures has an interesting, though relatively unexplored, history in psychology and psychoanalysis. Jung's famous "house-dream" (1995, pp.182-3) led him to infer the existence of a collective unconscious. "It was plain to me," he said, "that the house represented a kind of image of the psyche" (ibid, p.184). In the dream Jung descends through several layers of a house, each floor associated with a different historical period. He moves from the most recent civilised period, situated on the upper floor, through the ground floor, which dates from the fifteenth and sixteenth centuries, then down through the cellar representing the mediaeval period back to Roman times. Finally he arrives, via a stone staircase, into a cave, which signals to him on awakening "the prehistorical basis of the psyche" (ibid, p.184). Hitchcock's *Psycho* has the various levels of the Bates Motel modelled on the tripartite structure of the Freudian psyche. Griffin (1997) sees in Jung's account not evidence for archaic psychic structures but testimony of Jung's waking preoccupations with the relationship between psychology and history. Jung's theorising of the collective uncon-scious was not altogether amiss. The mistake was to envisage it as some immaterial metaphysical entity that patrolled the interface between mind and brain to give us memory beyond our individual experience rather than as the sum total of collective historical and cultural relations. Boym speaks of a "space of cultural memory" (2001, p.293), which lives on in the structure and content of the language we speak (and how we speak it), the behaviours we learn in our families, the identities we select (and which are selected for us), the myths and stories we tell one another, the possibilities (and impossibilities) we envisage for ourselves and others, and our sense of what kind of things, events and actions are believable and real and which are not.

Perhaps Jung can be forgiven for imputing a phantas-magorical quality to the psyche. Maybe it is inevitable that the transmission of the unlimited past into the present, barely graspable in any concrete manner beyond two to three genera-tions, can only be imagined via such ghostly referents while still retaining something of a human quality; not the ghost in the machine but the ghost beyond the machine. In a very real sense the phenomenon of "hauntings" may itself be a facet of the human mind's propensity to reach into the past – the past that is still reachable – to understand the present.

The space of the human interior has its own affective geography as well as symbolic structure, and how we arrange, organise and relate to the various objects that occupy it says much about how our psychic life is inseparable from the spaces we live and breathe in. This is true whether in a functional, artistic or emotional capacity. The temporal relationships we build with them – i.e. whether relating to the lived past, the imagined past or presently inhabited time – also says something about our relationship with material objects that goes well beyond the limits that Marxist thought could imagine, when it reduced our relationship with manufactured objects to one of commodity fetishism. Marx, though, did at least confer some importance on our relationship with inanimate matter: psychoanalysis surprisingly has largely neglected it. Only Winnicott (1951) explored the restricted class of objects, capable in childhood of functioning as transitional objects, which defensively occupy the terrain between the young child's psychic reality and the threatening external world – a half-way house between pure subjectivity and objectivity. But capitalism itself perpetually abolishes the lines between subjectivity and objectivity – invading our private spheres of desire with commercially inspired hungers and wants. Just where do we draw the line between the imperatives of our life and those of the market? This may be a question no one can answer until and unless the empire of the market is consigned to history.

As indicated in the previous chapter, Boym's work on the phenomenology of the urban interior tells us much about how these issues speak to matters of our physical, cultural and emotional survival in the rapidly changing world of the modern. The latter is the precondition for our problematic relationship with linear time, our subsequent invention of tradition and the inevitability of nostalgia. As Orwell knew well, and as Starosta (2007, p.157) observes, "the locus of ethical resistance" may often reside in small things – objects, isolated thoughts and piecemeal recollections. Such resistance is seldom geared to the impossible arrest of time but to the disappearance of values, affects, memories and truths. Objects then are never just objects and carry infinitely more than simply monetary value or even surplus value – being tangible aesthetic mementoes of our survival and our necessary psychological investment in the material world. As such they are reflections and signifiers of identity – speaking to us of our place and our history in the world. In this capacity they mediate our relationships to other persons, objects and entities both tangible and intangible. We use the variety of "things" we encounter to instruct us in the nature of the world we live in and its degree of permanence/impermanence. That is, we make and fashion the world at large as an "objective" one – i.e. saturated with things whose "object-ivity" makes the world existent. The durability of objects –exemplified by the special class of "antiques" – holds out the unfulfilled promise that time's imperatives may be resisted or at least postponed. Objects, unless broken or visibly decayed, radiate the appearance of stasis, opposing the flow of time. Events on the other hand and particularly those we locate in the natural world, seem fleeting, arising, progressing and passing. As we sit in the safe confines of our tranquil urban homes mentally deploying objects (conceptual and figural) to fix and know the world, we may thereby make it harder to envisage the world as one in unending flux. This may matter when it comes to trying to change it, whether the project is envisaged as re-building the world in its entirety or re-directing a fluid one.

Despite the manifest durability of the objective world and the apparent stasis of solid matter, entropy does its work, aided, abetted or resisted by human action. In time the outer world is transformed either through unimpeded decay, planned reconstruction, or planned or accidental destruction. The unending metamorphosis of the material world is where subjectivities and objectivities tantalisingly intertwine, one outcome of which is the vanishing materiality of the ruin, coeval with a vanishing consciousness of the past. Whilst fossils and ruins constitute the subject matter of distinct academic disciplines – one well-established, the other nascent (see Hell & Schönle, 2010) – our primary interest here is with their common psychogeographic significance. Our relationship to the "ruined" world is ambiguous. On one hand we seek to preserve ancient artefacts and monuments in a pickled cultural historical space which speaks to our collective (or ethno-national) human heritage – enabling partial answers to questions of origins and identity. On the other hand we idolise the shock of the modernist new. In one fundamentalist variant of this, the historicity of past relics – both physical ruins and established customs – can pose challenges to religious and political ontologies. In a profoundly anti-modern orgy, both the Khmer Rouge and ISIS, for example, have sought to reset their respective cultural clocks to an imagined year zero by cleansing the land of inconvenient historically situated human beings in the first case and in the second historical monuments along with human beings and their feared beliefs.

This desire to reset the past runs through psychotherapy as well as politics. Freud sought to counter this with his insistence on the acceptance of habitual neurotic misery as the best we can hope for – but in this he was hardly successful and the hope that the psychological clock can be reset and our pained and "ruined" self banished forever is pervasive. Though we carry and perpetually display our experiential "ruins," often enough we do so less than willingly.

The ruins of modernity threaten the intrusion of undesirable thoughts and memories of an altogether different kind to those of antiquity. They challenge the teleology of progress and perpetual modernisation that we in the West have been imprinted with. A ruin, whether physical or psychological, signals not only a future not realised, an alternative history gone begging, but also the inevitability of change in this age. The continuous erosion and reconstruction of landscape advances like a dream or a nightmare depending on one's political and psychological affiliations and whether one's own abode is demolished in the forward march of progress. Nothing stays the same but not everything progresses. This off-modern snapshot of simultaneous destruction, preservation and reconstruction is Benjamin's "dialectic at a standstill"; the past never relinquished, the future always anticipated but never arriving, the present moment missed.

I confess to recalling my own image of the future in the midst of the 1960s. It promised much and even now leaves a tangible nostalgia for what has never been. We all stand in some psychological relation to this whether we like it or not. As Boym notes, the problem with ruins is that "their meaning cannot be controlled" (2010b, p.83). Perhaps "ruinophilia" occupies the Western mind because its insistence on the decay of the physical reminds us that the life of the mind is ultimately dependent on the life of the body. Our naïve individual belief, born of the miracle of consciousness, is that we can go on forever. Our naïve cultural belief is that our way of life will similarly proceed unhindered. We know neither is true, hence the propensity of objects to stir reflexive longings – in fear, envy, resentment and nostalgia. Ruins, as Hell and Schönle (2010, p.8) note, cannot but "evoke the great levelling universality of death." The temporality of objects means that in addition to their manifest physical, material and immediate relational properties, they also carry a physical and aesthetic historical signature of the age in which they were "born." They are material expressions of a zeitgeist long after the winds of time have blown through it. It is this latter propensity which may stir the spirit of nostalgics[25] – of both restorative and reflective hues – as well as the fetish and acquisitive ardour of collectors of antiques, fighting impossibly against the certainties of entropy and our own demise from the world. "You can't take nothing with you but your soul," as John Lennon sang.

Then there is the belief that objects have the ability to protect their owner from harm; warding off evil spirits for example has a long history in all human cultures. Their success in doing so can be no less than the contemporary aspiration that we may be simultaneously reminded of, and protected against, the ravages of time. Our scientific theories in some ways can also be considered as amulets – prized possessions to ward off the chaos, unpredictability and impermanence of the world. But in reality they have limited success, for all the magical power invested in them by the scientific community. Compared to the ubiquitous and impermanent nature of the real, they function only in very limited domains concerned with a variety of transient structures and forms. To take but one example – and a pertinent one in matters of time – developmental psychology, as it is taught, appears largely unable to deal with life beyond the age at which we acquire a mastery of our native tongue, as if the ceaseless ebb and flow of change in human life effectively ended here, confined to young children. In the land of theory, reality must be fixed, categorised and arrested, or it would be culpable of the crime of perpetual fluency. Maybe this is because once we are linguistically fluent and able to speak for ourselves scientific method really doesn't know what to do with us. Psychology always has had too little to say about our irresistible movement through time – and about the sense we make of this as we meander toward our eventual encounter with mortality, the second certain fact of life after birth.

The mystery of life is really two mysteries, the seemingly abrupt events that punctuate it at its boundaries: the perplexing appearance of consciousness, and its equally perplexing disappearance, which is our point of departure into Shakespeare's "dateless night." Laing referred to death as an "essential baffling mystery" (cited in Kirsner, 2015, p.151), something that we could only truly know about, as opposed to observe, if we could remember having died. These unfathomable movements of consciousness to and from the world never yield their secrets to rational thought. The boundary conditions however are not mirror images. Our lives begin with a miraculous appearance but following our disappearance the attendant waves stirred by our existence continue to reverberate across the times and places of others, carrying social forms of memory, intelligence, emotion and behaviour, all overlooked forms of intergenerational continuity. These events are embedded within the greater total mystery of being. How could the universe arise from nothing? How could it be eternal? Though these two options seem to exhaust the ontological conditions for the existence of the world, neither is capable of comprehension. In Gödel's terms they denote undecidable propositions. For Kant they denote the limits of pure reason. Neither possibility is thus primed for capture within the limits set by our propensity and ability for story-telling. Since the Enlightenment we have remained content that the world we experience is the product of some grand causal tale, having convinced ourselves that the triumph of scientific reason entails a truth that all reality is amenable to reason. But this isn't the case and why should it be when the boundary conditions of our being signpost both the limits of reason and the limits of what is knowable? Knowledge too lives within four walls and beyond its horizons lies the unknown dangerous world into which, as Blake recognised, we must leap, with or without articles of faith. The map is not the territory. The mystery is not made any the less mysterious by any leap of faith. The space of the mysterious in it strictest sense lies beyond not only both faith and reason but also the imagined chaos that these systems of thought seek to tame.

The social and symbolic space furnished by any home – and systems of thought are certainly places where we take up residence – affords protection against this feared chaos and uncertainty that lurks unrepentant outside. Through the life of the objects that exist within it, the anarchy of the changing world is contained, though the manner of this containment is dynamic, the various *objets d'art* of the interior conveying a range of co-existing temporalities through which the inhabitants of that space are connected to past and future lives. "To live," Walter Benjamin wrote, "means to leave traces." All objects carry such traces and thus are part of a social life, links in a vast narrative topography. That these objects may too play a mediating role in the continuation of patterns of behaviour across generations has yet to stir the minds of researchers who for the most part remain in awe of the projected prowess of biological determinism.

Beyond the house, however, parallels between psychic interiority and urban interiority have also largely escaped attention (see Boym, 2001, p.175 and p.212 for a couple of interesting examples). This is most likely because the connections between urban structures (the streets, thoroughfares, railways and roads of the metropolis) would call attention to the overwhelming importance of the social as well as our relationship to the monumental landscape, both of which lure attention away from the individualised psyche – the desired subject/object in all schools of analysis as well as academic psychology. In her poetic reverie on getting lost, Rebecca Solnit goes substantially further than Jung and posits a resemblance between the city and the conscious mind – a network to "calculate, administrate, manufacture" (2006, pp.88-9). The underbelly of the city – its ruins – then become its unconscious, the source that brings it to life, a wilderness "full of promise of the unknown," its "memory," "darkness" and "lost lands." In such imaginative vistas our urban exteriors are extensions of us, the boundaries of the self, far-reaching and out into infinity; an infinitude of bricks, mortar, concrete and green space, replete with gendered identity (cities are invariably assigned feminine identities, perhaps because of the life they house within) reveries, hopes and history. Like us the city is born, grows and aspires to a kind of immortality. Like us its constituent elements are eventually returned to dust.

Everyday use of language is full of examples of how we draw on the formal architecture and topography of the city to elucidate psychological states and conditions of life. We speak, for example, of "tunnel vision," of being at a "dead end," or up a "cul-de-sac," of things being "a two-way street," of reaching "milestones," "landmarks" or "crossroads" in one's life, of being "driven up the wall," of "backs against the wall," "drinking in the last-chance saloon," of "life in the fast lane," looking for a "direction in life," "going off the rails," "feeling like a wreck" or "going down memory lane," etc. Solnit (2014, p.6) draws from this the conclusion that the mind too is like a landscape, and physical movement with the body through space is simultaneously a journey through its contours and valleys. Perhaps our travels through the entirety of physical space, including the cosmos, are simultaneously travels through our mind – as well as journeys to meet ourselves – a point Boym (2003) considers in her discussion of Russian conceptions of both consciousness and the cosmos.

Our psychic life has structured not only the entirety of the world in terms of what we can perceive in three-dimensions but also our own passageway through life, a one-way journey along the unidimensional arrow of time, even if our experience sometimes tells us otherwise. Only in art and psychotherapy do we go forward in life by going backwards in time. Our psychogeography[26] takes in both the forms and contents of city life and extends through the symbolic and memorial significance of specific locations and passageways through it. To practise psycho-geography is to invite and map a flux of memory and emotion – reveries, desires, dreams, daydreams, impressions, hopes, fears, plays, longings, joys and sorrows – against the changing physical backdrop of the journey or specific genius loci. How we are influenced by (and in turn influence) the form, content and symbolic richness of the spaces we inhabit and traverse will depend upon the time and the manner in which we occupy them. It depends, for example on whether that is as walker,[27] runner, driver, cyclist, wheelchair user, worker, shopper, native, migrant, tourist, stranger, wanderer, exile, homeless person, protestor, writer, street artist, photographer or filmmaker. It also depends on the various relationships, motivations, intentions, inclinations and moods we bring in these different capacities, to say nothing of our physical, mental and economic propensities. Our gaze upon the urban interior thus extends immeasurably beyond the singular romantic or collective tourist mode of apprehension (Urry, 2006).

The manner of our occupation and our purpose may, in addition, challenge existing social codes or cross legal boundaries and be undertaken under diverse states of mind (e.g. shaped by drugs or hunger). Each of these will engage our memorial and imaginative capabilities in diverse ways and may contribute in turn to a progressive imprinting of mood and history in specific locales for future adventurers and visitors to imbibe. Just as social spaces become "environments of memory" (Bondi, Davidson & Smith, 2005, p.9) they also become environments of affect – practised and fixed in transitory moments and broad swathes of time as much by a cloud of semantic associations as by Cartesian coordinates. The city is a living museum, an unbounded evolving repository of history made and in the making.

Our visions of both the past and the future (utopian/dystopian/myopian) will to some degree be grounded in our contemporary psychogeographical landscape: the places we haunt and are haunted by and the emotional attachments to journeys undertaken, whether uniquely, irregularly or frequently. This constant saturation of public space with private meaning and the reciprocal invasion of private space with public meaning suggests that any attempt to draw a firm line between the two realms can never be more than social convention. We must always inhabit both – a fact that is instructive about the artificiality and instability of border disputes between psychological and social scientific work. Within the human dimension, places have no properties above and beyond the meaning of the lives that are inscribed in and around them and that leak into the world through time. Particular places and situations moreover are more obviously subject to the porous interchange of public and private meaning – notably those related to our health, well-being and legal status when and where our personal autonomy has become a concern for others. Hospitals, jails and courthouses have always been places of immense psychological and social significance, waystations of fear, anticipation, captivity and freedom.

Cities are simultaneously both real and imagined spaces, oscillating perennially between the virtual and the actual, the factual and physical in a dialectical dance with the metaphysical and the magical – an eternal confluence of reassuring banality and unsettling unfamiliarity. Such are the means by which we transmit the delicate fruits of history to those who come after us. If, as Calvino said, "desires are already memories" (1997, p.7), then we daily walk through the long-lost dreams of those whose footsteps came before us as we inscribe our own presence on the dreams of others still to come. Forms of the city also exist in the imaginary spaces of our dreams – the unreal places of disjunctive unsettling familiarity in which our night-time thoughts, wishes and worries are realised in an unfolding drama of virtual interaction and emotion as our mental landscape is explored, probed, ordered, rearranged and hopefully put to bed. The city then, like our psychic interiority, resonates with an infinity of symbolic possibilities, never precisely the same from one day to the next.

Social scientists employ the concept of intersubjectivity to help us navigate through the confluence (and divergence) of meanings in a relational space which helps us to define, build and experience social reality. But there is no satisfactory term to embrace the flux and network of relationships that over time connect people, memory, affect, objects, land and landscape, and which through their delicate synchrony and resonance constitute a much fuller and more expansive reality. Some in the arena of human geography (see Conradson, 2005) have suggested that an ecological framework provides a fitting frame of reference to contemplate this reality. Though the notion possesses certain advantages, marking as its subject matter the myriad interactions between organisms and environment, it does nothing to suggest an expansion/projection of the experiential realm (usually considered to exist *within* organisms) into or onto the outward world of material things. Daniel Miller sees in our relations with people and objects the possibility of an "ethnography of enchantment" (2009, p.31), where we prime our research with a poetic and almost magical-realist methodology. Such enchantment could spin a variety of semantic tales latent in the word, to produce a state of pleasure and elation in the act of conducting research – thereby ignoring the prescriptions for emotional detachment demanded by tradition – and to produce a state of metamorphosis in those we research; to reveal something latent and precious in the subject through the spell of human interaction. Miller's research aesthetic undoubtedly carries some of the unconventional and off-modern character of Boym's, recognising the poverty of post-modern frameworks for grasping the diversity of actual human existence and the multiple asynchronous beats of cultural time that give it rhythm and defy a totalising linear narrative. Not for the first time is our language problematic, for what is at issue is not only the universal inevitability of at best partial truths but the inseparability of our supposedly inner and outer worlds.

The changing external world of material objects is in a very real sense saturated with the imprint and consequences of experience. One can think of this as a defining facet of city life. Experience, memory and imagination are everywhere inscribed into it. One can always turn this on its head and see the inner experiential realm as reflective of the connectivity that exists between material objects out there in the world, the world as introjected rather than psychically projected. But this too presupposes a barrier between inner and outer which in practice and in scientific terms is hard to justify. Perhaps part of the problem lies in the exclusion of subjectivity from the natural scientific realm – the presupposition against anything seemingly "immaterial" acting as a driving force behind the evolution of organisms and their environments. Consciousness here remains a problem not just in psychology but in the broader life sciences. It resists capture as an operationally measurable and effective variable at large within the material world, despite the abundant evidence that intelligence has evolved throughout the biological world and has been a mighty factor in shaping its evolution. Our theorising of the human condition seeks to "avoid [this] logic of the cutting edge" (Boym, 2010c) and is intended to unfold in the interstices between inner and outer, between subjectivity and objectivity, bridging, conjoining or abolishing such dualities, leaving a place where we are not constrained by the direction or angle of the gaze. This is to go beyond the choice between an inward and outward gaze. As Sartre maintained, consciousness is always relational – neither the world nor the self is privileged or dispensable from our standpoint. We remain intertwined with the world, neither the ghost nor the machine.

Already understood by philosophers, psychoanalysts and social psychologists as relational, the self, whatever we mean by it, is thereby decentred, its multi-directional relations physically stamped into a world imbued with meaning, "logos and pathos, memory and imagination" (Boym, ibid) – a conjoint mental-physical reality subject to the pulsating and decaying rhythms of time. The self, envisaged from this vantage point, is everywhere and nowhere, at once singular and universal, not so much post-modern as off-modern, a dynamical human field permeating and saturating the places of the world we inhabit. The geography of this field is littered alternatively with the walls and bridges (actual and metaphoric) we habitually erect, either to divide and compartmentalise humanity or to reconnect with hope its disparate elements and divisions into one. Thus do our social spaces reveal at one and the same time the expansion and dissolution of the self.

Coverley (2010, p.85) recalls the maps etched in the mind of Gilles Ivain, a member of the Lettrist International who went by the nom de plume of Chtcheglov. Ivain described "entire cities, their districts corresponding to 'the whole spectrum of diverse feelings that one encounters *by chance* in everyday life. Bizarre Quarter – Happy Quarter (specially reserved for habitation) – Noble and Tragic Quarter (for good children) – Historical Quarter (museums, schools) – Useful Quarter (hospital, tool shops) – Sinister Quarter etc.'" Were Ivain still alive today one wonders how he would have mapped the financial district of the City of London – perhaps as the "Destructive Quarter" or the "Ocean Quarter of Infinite Greed," born of a historical tsunami upon the surrounding islands of the poor and dispossessed. Ivain's maps are the summation and transposition of his own passageways through the urban sprawl – and so are unique to him. In any journey through the city we meet, pass, avoid, bump into the bearers of an incalculable number of other such mappings – some more well-formed than others. They are a succession of hypothetical realities which may never interface, save the possibility of one person asking another the way – this a long-lost function of British police officers, before they discovered the more dangerous possibilities of beating people up and shooting unarmed Brazilian electricians on the London Underground, an act in the new geography of security-state control. Space may in fact be psychologically mapped in innumerable ways – by desire, fear, boredom, desperation, hope, escape, adventure, etc. – and these mappings may be intrinsically oppositional, so that what may be a zone of desire for some (e.g. males) may be simultaneously a zone of fear or trepidation for others (e.g. females); or, to take another example, the places of privation or boredom for the socially marginalised may be of intrinsic interest and curiosity for those motivated by research or a predilection for reflection on life's great lottery. Privilege produces untold psychological skews in the world.

We are then creatures of imagined space and imagined times, our lives etched into every nook and cranny of both. *The Bonzo Dog Do Dah Band*'s pop anthem "I'm the Urban Spaceman," a psychedelic hymn to the confluence of '60s drug culture, the space race and post-war urban regeneration, plays with this notion. The song's writer, Neil Innes, reasoned that if there were "urban spaces," as the war-damaged areas were then known, ergo there must be urban spacemen inhabiting them, their space walks no doubt aided and abetted by the pharmacologically assisted reimagining of the urban environment; "Zebracrossings made of lilies / Belishabeacons made of orangeblossom / Busstops huge irises / Traffic lights made of snapdragons" (Henri, 1967, p.34). Ewen MacColl's ode to working-class life and love, "Dirty Old Town," imagined the city in a different tone and speaks poignantly to life in the industrial yesteryear and a future still to be forged, intimately connecting love, landscape, work, life, hope and regret.

MacColl had a feel for the emotional microcosm of urban space, a tender regard for the details in life, the "asides of the spirit" (Boym, 2001, p.281) that matter, conjoined with openness to the bright possibilities and pains of human existence. MacColl's better-known works[28] constitute a veritable ecology of the human heart. There are no more dirty old towns in the fading ruins of Britain's industrial landscape. Waves of de-industrialisation and global movements of capital have seen to that – with the hearts of the communities they depended on simultaneously vanishing with them or at best relocated into dispersed fragments of disjointed longings. The spaces they occupied have become homes to constellations of quite different meaning. Remembrance of their time has not so much faded as been catapulted into oblivion, erased by hypermarkets, television, mass underemployment, fast-cut camera movements, the digital age, ubiquitous technologies of surveillance and anomie, fear and despair on every street corner. All eyes are on the present as alien elusive possibilities from the past are eased away from our conscious grasp and dreams and memories are devoured by the prying eyes of accelerated programmed forgetfulness.

At this point in human history urbanity constitutes the dominant mode of human existence. But of course this was not always so. In pre-history humans brought their fledging psycho-geographies of nature into the burgeoning new worlds of enclosed space. The tale of our expulsion from Eden ends only as the history of our entrapment in the town or city begins. Into it we bring a foundational mental architecture with which we map the chaotic expanding space of human settlements and the journeys within, to and from them. The fabled dialectic of human nature and nurture can be said to begin here with human settlement – the wildness of nature projected simultaneously beyond the city walls and interiorised in the hearts of men and women. The city as nature is then lost and with this loss comes a different rhythm of life and perception of time.

A generation of people now inhabit a reduced temporal zone of referential experience in which a few years before their birth is considered almost ancient history. Even now, scarcely a few decades after the Holocaust, we remain numb and hardly aware of the colossal and reverberating damage that this huge nightmare unleashed upon the entirety of humanity, Jews and non-Jews alike. It is a profound mistake to see the events of the 1930s and '40s as an issue for Jewish people only. To connect with this and take on board its significance as a serious psychological issue would require us to acknowledge that the nature and depth of our connection to other people and to our surrounds transcends both time and place and is a part of every person's life history.

A psychology worth its salt must retain a sensitivity to this if it is to avoid accusations of irreverence, to say nothing of irrelevance, insensitivity or ineptitude. The sweep of what is to be included within its fold could incorporate whatever gives us purpose, whatever propels us through and stands with us in the transitory moments of our existence, both alone and with others. Songs, hymns, spirituals, dance, drama, prose, poetry, massage, music, meditation and a myriad other forms of action in the world belong in psychology – not as objects of study but as forms of action, aspects of the human condition, ways of interrogating reality about the meaning of our lives and constituting the realities of them. Our actions are simultaneously questions and answers. They have an off-modern "quality of improvisation," they are conjectures "that don't distort the facts but explore their echoes, residues, implications, shadows" (Boym, 2010c). The spaces that traditional psychology has closed to reflection and contemplation are often where the human in our natures is most keenly felt and elaborated and where what is of most interest awaits.

Jung's *Red Book* – his personal account of his adventures and experiments behind the veils of his "mythopoetic imagination" – throws a different light on his life's labour. In this work, published for the first time over forty years after his death, he sought, both literally and metaphorically, to open the mouth of the dead – to enter the dateless night and bring the weight of human history into the work of psychology, as both experience and practice – in order that we be fully acquainted with the transgenerational imprimatur that is an integral part of our reality whether we are consciously aware of it or not. It is of considerable interest that in this quest Jung nowhere referred to this work as psychology, perhaps realising that the discipline of the soul had already become too narrow.[29] Hillman sees in Jung's visionary text the seeds of an enterprise that of necessity suggested a "dramatic, aesthetic, poetic, artistic" form of practice (Hillman & Shamdasani, 2013, p.14) which would be necessary to come to terms with the nature of psychological reality in any meaningful way. Shamdasani considered such a practice would be contingent upon abandoning psychology as a scientific quest for knowledge and returning it to the field of the arts. These are ways of knowing ourselves and one another, ways of articulating the human condition that deviate from the accepted mores of academic psychology. How was it that these were ever omitted when it came to the quest to understand ourselves in the world? Jung was prepared to cross temporal, cultural, experiential and academic boundaries to try and make sense of his own life as well as others'. Boym's work in the off-modern vernacular has, curiously enough, undertaken the same journey, taking an equally imaginative and diverse path to the frontiers of our horizons – including our relation to the cosmos (Boym, 2003). We learn from them that making sense of the world requires making sense of our own places in it. It can never be an impersonal task.

Both tell us that a radical re-visioning of psychology is possible if we are prepared to consider biographical and autobiographical narrative across these same expanses and avoid privileging the psychological above other frames of reference; in fact, avoid privileging any framework at all and mistaking narrative for only that which can be committed to the electronic or material page. With this we should not at all expect that an off-modern psychology will be recognisable to those who practise the current version. The off-modern invites reflection – perhaps a nostalgic reflection for a vision of the human, one not beholden to the eighteenth-century Romantic awe of emotion as uncritical guide to wild nature. This reflection could be a radical re-imagining of the importance of human relationships in situ – one not confined to our relationships to one another or to our individual selves, but extending to the cosmologies and geographies we inhabit, both large and small. Everything from our nascent appreciation of the night sky, to the places we call home and the people with whom we feel at home; a genealogy of relationships that reach out in space and time, to connect objects, people and places through actions, thoughts and feelings. The prominence accorded to relationships and experience here are fundamental to the notion of psychogeography being developed and its place within an off-modern psychology. Capra (2015) sees an emphasis on these twin conceptual pillars as establishing the epistemological basis for a holistic challenge to the entire reductionist paradigm of classical science. Capra himself, in works such as *The Tao of Physics* (1975) and *The Turning Point* (1982), has been elaborating a scientific world view which is itself decidedly off-modern.

In the following chapter I will turn my attention to the arts of psychotherapy and how our current frameworks for trying to put right what has gone wrong in human relationships can be estranged – given an off-modern twist. The arts, as age-old means to come to terms with the human condition – including the arts of psychotherapy and being "optimally" human – are a vital adjunct to self-knowledge. In the following chapter there will be more to say about this.

The roughest roads are not found across rivers and mountains, but in people's hearts
– Bai Juyi (cited in Shan, 2002, p.32)

Five

Estrangement, Psychotherapy and Counselling

My tears are like the quiet drift
Of petals from some magic rose;
And all my grief flows from the rift
Of unremembered skies and snows
– Dylan Thomas (2003, p.258)

There is no better start to thinking than laughter
– Walter Benjamin (2007, p.236)

The Therapeutic Encounter

Since Freud's day the types and varieties of psychotherapy – along with its erstwhile and indistinguishable cousin, counselling – have multiplied. Accompanying this seemingly endless expansion has been an explosion of research seeking to pinpoint exactly what it is about the process of psychotherapy that is responsible for producing effective change in the lives of clients. With regard to this goal, some commentators (e.g. Stratton, 2015) have questioned the usefulness of a research paradigm rooted in the natural sciences, which invites a transformation of the therapeutic human encounter into a series of identifiable and quantifiable variables whose precise effects can be teased out through careful and deliberate external control. Without denying that some of this research has been useful, the most frequently cited results from it point to the chief "ingredient" being the nature of the relationship between client and therapist – which returns us to the question of what it is that makes human relationships worthwhile and cherishable; what enriches our lives in any encounter with another person? This is the flipside of the coin to the dark matter of what diminishes and damages our lives with others.

Rather than revisiting, then, the main alleyways and byways of the psychotherapeutic research literature, I wish to adopt a different perspective, that we may literally see psychotherapy differently – a lateral move on my part to reconfigure perception of the business and practice of psychotherapy. One of the assumptions at the forefront of psychotherapy research is that it involves the application of some esoteric skill – embodied and cultivated in the therapist, accumulated through years of training and supervision – which works upon the individual who has sought help. Like a matryoshka doll, this assumption itself contains another: that the iron test of whether psychotherapy is a worthy endeavour depends on there being an outcome, an endpoint that can be considered successful – that in some way our suffering has been relieved and we can be said to "feel" better. Nested within this is yet another assumption: that psychotherapy is quite unlike real life and is best considered separate from it. This is probably due in some small part to the fact that we enter the world without formal or practical knowledge of human relationships and most of us go through life without receiving any.

My starting point is to hold all these assumptions in abeyance and to rethink the contours of fruitful human relationships. In referring to fruitfulness, care must be taken not to fall prey to the Manichean ideas of outcome found in the research literature, suggesting a clear determinable "positive" consequence. I have in mind nothing more than how to live well – the age-old question posed by Aristotle, which it need hardly be said does not suggest a clear specifiable consequence. Living well is predicated of course on the more fundamental tenet of how to live at all – the necessity to circumvent, avoid, confront or head off the perennial dangers to one's existence. Life in the West however seems to be predicated on a different notion: that the impediments to a risk-free life can be eliminated and that we should seek to create a world in which external threats – whether social, physical, biological or psychological – are vanquished, leaving us to live out a quiet existence in some corner of the world in a perpetual state of dull or satiated happiness. A version of this is perhaps exemplified in Huxley's *Brave New World*. Paradoxically, within this utopian, risk-free, pleasure-saturated universe, political norms dictate that we be left to confront economic risk, uncertainty and inequality as if these were forces of nature – red in tooth and claw. The end of history was never meant to signal the end of free-market economics. The new economics of happiness is really about the happiness that money brings to the few or the resigned artificial happiness of doing nothing to disturb the status quo. The fault lines of such representations tell us much about the world we inhabit or at least have come to believe we inhabit.

To live well is not to turn off the tap of human feeling in one direction while we are permitted to experience it in another; it involves an active appreciation of the vitality of all existence – the painful as well as the joyful. It is notable that Shklovsky saw estrangement as a means to return such vitality to one's experience of the world – that it would make the fear of war more real and one's wife more lovable (see Boym, 2010, p.207). This might suggest that the affective possibilities of existence always point in two directions, but perhaps it is more than that – that a joy in living permeates all experience even whilst suffering. Our predilections for construing the world in terms of binary opposites – a cornerstone of Kelly's theory of personal constructs – make it difficult to appreciate that this may be so. Kelly proposed that we anticipate the world to come through a uniquely personal network of such binaries, but there is nothing magical about the number two and no reason experience should respect its boundaries. That is not to imply that the co-presence of suffering with joy means that we take pleasure in suffering – but that one may still experience the joy of existence even when suffering. The confusion engendered by unexpected suffering (and is not all suffering unexpected at the moment it transpires?) of course allows for the possibility that pain and pleasure may form a confusing duet, though it hardly needs saying that there are multiple pathways to such confusion.

The pleasures of existence are often brought into focus following bereavement or its anticipation, when the significance of the "ordinary marvellous" is elevated to a pivotal place in our consciousness. The sense that the miracle of conscious experience, the pleasure of being in the world, is for another person no more, or may soon be no more, or that the possibility of our direct experience of the world with them has ceased, just as eventually this will be the case for all of our experience, heightens our sense of the majesty and wonder of our existent days. The ordinary becomes extraordinary, infused with magic. This "time out of time" in the midst our earthly existence, Boym argued, is the best we can hope for – temporally bounded adventure in which we abandon ourselves to the "powers and accidents of the world," permitting us to "embrace the cosmos beyond [...] immediate experience" (2008, pp.6-7). The fruits of such adventure call to mind Maslow's concept of peak experiences, linked to his concept of self-actualisation. But whereas Boym, Benjamin and Baudelaire locate the experience as a relational unpremeditated encounter with life's possibilities, Maslow's conception has come to resemble a personality predisposition, hermetically sealed within the walls of the individual, a characteristic one can pursue, cultivate and acquire in the race to become moral top dog. Perhaps the problem lies more with psychology's propensity to detach, de-contextualise and reify both the person and the world than Maslow's initial attempts to articulate something of importance. Vitz (1994) saw in the psychological community's wider appropriation of "self-actualisation," the transformation of a descriptive notion into a moral norm and with it a serious misreading of the adventurous human possibilities in a dazzlingly complex world.

The structure of modern life, left out of the equation by the theoreticians of self-actualisation, renders it more difficult to zoom in on this sense of ordinary wonder, but it can be a key feature of a psychotherapeutic encounter – a part of ensuring the client (and indeed the therapist) is ready to deal with the business at hand. It is preparation for the task ahead – that they are both immersed in the present moment with a measure of free attention to face what needs facing. This can involve calling attention to present sensory experience, or those aspects of one's current life that are going well – however small they may seem. Kaufman & New (2004, p.58) refer to the presence or gathering of such free attention as a key factor in making counselling effective. This is especially so when both therapist and client can revel in it, when their intelligences can conjoin unimpaired by the pull of any distress in their lives.

This points to the therapeutic encounter as a fluid entity; it is not a question of something being fixed in one person but of a relationship which is temporarily directed to enhancing the quality of (at least) one person's life. Many in the profession speak of the encounter as enhancing their own lives. Psychotherapy then is always an act of co-creation, so that strictly speaking there is no therapeutic outside to bring about a therapeutic change inside. What appears outside (i.e. the therapist) because of the relational character of the encounter is necessarily a part of what is "inside" the client. As Laing wrote in *Knots*, "one is on the outside of one's own inside" (1971b, p.83). In as much as a natural science of behaviour is incapable of seeing this, a natural science of psychotherapy is problematic.

It is to be considered unfortunate and indeed somewhat perplexing that the literature on the topic of estrangement is virtually unknown in psychotherapy circles, as its relevance to what goes on in the course of it is plentiful. Estrangement, like psychotherapy, can be considered in numerous ways, one of which is as an attempt to disrupt the automatisation of daily life. As Boym notes, estrangement is theorised as a means for disrupting the "monster of everyday routine," captured in the Russian language as "byt" (2010, p.331). Estrangement then, like psychotherapy, is an approach, a practice intended to bring about change in the manner and tone of living – specifically to bring about change in the way one feels about the world even when some actions against a source of tyranny may not be practically possible. This simultaneous unsettling of the behavioural, cognitive and affective makes it something more than deconstruction and of greater significance than any appreciation of the importance of counterfactual realities in cognitive science would suggest (see for example Hofstadter, 1981). Indeed the failure of cognitive and experimental psychology to satisfactorily accommodate emotion in its mechanistic models of the human organism has been one of its biggest failings. Like psychotherapy, estrangement may be considered in terms of both form and content – though these may frequently be inextricably intertwined. Rogers for example provided his prescription for "successful" psychotherapy in terms of warmth, genuineness and empathy. Of course, devoid of any specific act, gesture or meaning imparted by a therapist, these could be mistakenly understood as mere technique; but as mere technique, empathy cannot be empathy, nor can warmth or genuineness be genuine. Outside of prescriptive technique, estrangement like psychotherapy must be invented – hence its close ties to the arts – and this is perhaps a further reason why psychotherapy, at least where it has been allied to the moribund scientist-practitioner model, has been unlikely to (theoretically) encounter estrangement.

Regrettably, science and poetry seldom mix. Freud however did briefly touch upon a variety of estrangement in his essay on the uncanny (2003). Described as "one of his strangest" though "most compelling" works for its influence on subsequent literary criticism (Haughton, 2003, p.xlii-xliii), it traces the peculiar affective dread to a disturbance of one's habitual sense of reality, a de-familiarisation of what was once familiar, that owed its peculiar and fearful strangeness either to a return of repressed infantile conflicts or a resurfacing of once "primitive" beliefs surmounted in the course of acculturation. Freud's essay omits any consideration of the resemblance between these experiences of dread and the phenomenon of *déjà vu*, which he had previously also described as "uncanny" in *The Psychopathology of Everyday Life* (1975, p.329), and which he similarly attributes to the recollection of an unconscious (repressed) fantasy. Why one should evoke feelings of dread and the other nothing beyond mild curiosity is left untouched.

Freud considered that his brief treatise had "satisfied psychoanalytic interest in the problem" (ibid, p.16) and that what remained was an issue for aesthetics.[30] Others have however tackled it, more often than not in passing: Bion (see Potter, 2015) for example speculating that the origins of the sense lie either in intra-uterine experience or else, following Heidegger, in some concealed primal source of being. For Heidegger it was this uncanny sense – our estrangement from pure being – that provided the ontological basis for our openness to mystery. Kotsko (2015) in contrast tackles it full-on, making the uncanny – "creepiness" as he calls it – the centrepiece of the enigma of desire. In this take on the strange, all desire is non-normative and therefore transgressive of social norms. The bed-fellow to Kotsko's estrangement of desire in modern times is the computational metaphor of the human organism – an epistemological zone where desire is also transgressive – but the nature of the transgression is in this case different. In the computable human, what has been outlawed and rendered non-existent is the entirety of emotional life.

But why confine the uncanny to the drives? All told, the analysts have missed an opportunity to see the uncanny not as an isolated item of psychological interest but as a member of a much broader class of phenomena concerning the strangeness of existence, taking in but not limited to various forms of de-familiarisation, including de-realisation and de-personalisation. Had Freud done so, the entire range of problems brought to him in the course of his psychoanalytic career might have been considered as arriving on his doorstep at precisely that point in his patients' lives when their sense of the familiar and comfortable had been disturbed. Likewise psychoanalysis might then have been constructed not as "the royal road to the unconscious," but as a pathway to well-being built upon a practice of double estrangement: a merging of art and technique to estrange the estranged – to de-familiarise the unfamiliarity of existence and the familiarity of an individual's distress. But one encounters nothing like this throughout the field of psychoanalytic literature. What we are left with instead is the notion of the "talking cure" and the aim of rendering the unconscious, conscious – the familiarising of the unfamiliar, which purportedly leads one to insight. The edifice of psychoanalysis was of course built upon the notion of the unconscious; thus acquainting oneself with the unfamiliar is its pivotal analytic strategy. A strategy of estrangement towards one's troubles, though, does not require that their source be rooted in the unconscious.

Psychic Trauma or Distress?

Both human nature and the wider world of which we are a part can be considered as essentially benign, with human behaviour turning destructive only as a consequence of hurtful and painful experiences. In his *Studies on Hysteria* with Breuer, Freud originally referred to "psychic trauma" (Freud & Breuer, 2004) – but the phrase is unfortunate, carrying the etymological connotations of a physical wound, and as a result the question of whether the trauma is understood as the imposition of external events and stimuli or the responses to these is somewhat hazy. This is fully in keeping with the scientific orthodoxy of the day which gave *a priori* consideration to the physical; and of course the behaviourist tradition which was to follow exacerbated this considerably. In the eyes of some writers, not least Freud himself, the nascent psychoanalytic discipline, with its eyes now firmly fixed on the ubiquity of psychic trauma, was seen as reducing the strangeness of mental disorder while simultaneously elevating the strangeness of everyday mental life – which soon had its own "psycho" pathology. Whilst this had (and still has) the potential to undermine the concept of mental illness (after all, if the same processes underlie the supposedly normal, neurotic and psychotic, what is the *medical* point of distinguishing between them?) events took a different turn, and word soon had it that because of psychoanalysis everybody was now mentally ill.

The psychiatric profession has been trying to make good on the promise ever since. In physics, the same laws of motion apply equally to ballistic missiles and tennis balls – their relative disruption to the fabric of everyday life and the social approval or disapproval they evince is not a factor in how they are conceptualised, theorised or understood. The upshot of this is that the terms "mental disorder," "psychopathology" and "mental illness" correspondingly possess no explanatory value at all. There cannot be two classes of explanation for behaviours which are approved or disapproved, desired or undesired.

The term "distress" signals a different priority and a way out of the above impasse. It connotes a disturbance in one's well-being in the world – which may be manifest in unpleasant experiences and psychological states, or in habitual and repetitive patterns of behaviour. It is of more than passing interest that Breuer and Freud first defined psychic trauma in terms that make it quite clear that what is being considered is not in fact analogous to a physical wound and carries no further meaning beyond the effect of distress: "Any experience which gives rise to the distressing affects of fright, anxiety, shame or psychical pain can have this effect [...] and understandably it depends on the sensitivity of the person concerned [...] whether the *experience* will take on traumatic value" (ibid, p.9; italics mine). Psychic trauma then is merely distress writ large.

Cromby, Harper and Reavy (2013) note that this non-medicalised term permits no easy or straightforward discrimination between those who may require or solicit professional care and those who don't. Experiences of distress and suffering are part and parcel of the fabric of everyday life and hence are terms suitably applicable to everyone. What then does it mean to be distressed? The term is usually taken for granted and undefined. However, in co-counselling[31] we find a useful and clear operational definition. The co-counselling framework embodies a set of interlocking assumptions about the nature of reality, the nature of human beings, the nature of distress and recovery from it. Within this framework, what is conceptualised as distressing is anything that disturbs the normally smooth operation of our intelligence and shifts our usually flexible repertoire into a more rigid and mechanical mode of response. Under such adversity, the

normally discrete ensemble of perception, categorisation, anticipation and action which comprises our tailored response to each
moment of existence is disrupted and replaced with a mecha-
nised remembering (recording and modelling) of what
transpired. The remembering may be conscious or it may be
enacted behaviourally. In these distress recordings, each element
of an experience is capable of triggering any other. Sights,
sounds, smells, tactile, kinaesthetic and bodily sensations as well
as thoughts are treated as an undifferentiated whole. This leads
to the very real possibility that on any subsequent occasion in
which aspects of a new experience are judged to be similar to
those of an old distressing one, the earlier responses may be
triggered – a process referred to as re-stimulation. The resulting
behaviour under the influence of the distress is rigid and
inflexible; the desire to act out old patterns of behaviour may be
experienced as compulsive, irresistible and seemingly beyond
one's capacity to choose to do anything else. Distress recordings
thus substitute an old inaccurate picture of reality for what is
presently the case. What is evident in this account is that distress
is highly personal – depending on the model of the world one has
for interpreting and acting in it. It is a matter of what the world
means to each one of us.

Co-counselling theory proposes that the practical job of the
counsellor is to therefore challenge or contradict the meaningful
content of these distress recordings so that they are not mistaken
for reality. When this is done sufficiently, a process of emotional
discharge (laughter, crying, talking, raging, shaking, sweating,
yawning) takes place and is accompanied by a spontaneous
reprocessing and re-evaluation of the information originally
contained in the distress recording. With sufficient emotional
discharge and re-evaluation the distressed person (client) returns
to a flexible, more relaxed level of functioning. This practical job
of the counsellor to contradict distress is the point at which the
practice of co-counselling takes on a shape reminiscent of

Shklovsky's practices of estrangement. We might thus re-envision the practice as one in which the counsellor seeks to estrange the client's distress – i.e. to make it distant and strange, so that, to the client, it no longer represents reality or reflects who they are as a person. The processes of emotional discharge, enshrined as the centrepiece of co-counselling theory, bear more than a passing resemblance to the age-old concept of catharsis. If this theory is correct and these processes contribute, in no small degree, to liberating a client from the effects of past hurts, then it is of great importance to understand why the notion of catharsis within psychotherapy no longer has a central role.[32] To understand that, we need to understand how the concept entered psychotherapy in the first place, and, once there, how its original range and depth of meaning came to be transformed within the behavioural sciences at least[33] into the restricted and impoverished notion of simple individual emotional expression or even the mere completion of a psychological activity (see Hogg & Vaughan, 2010, p.235[34]) largely de-coupled either from any substantive cognitive and behavioural change or the social context in which it occurs.

This is key to understanding the contours of much psychotherapy as it now stands, as well as its development as a discipline since Freud, and why these practices of estrangement no longer occupy centre stage in the pantheon of psychotherapy and counselling. However, the question is of considerable importance beyond the realm of psychotherapy. Mention of the cathartic "purification of emotion" goes back to Aristotle in a context that is at once public and theatrical. One of the functions of dramatic art, Aristotle held, was to arouse emotions – principally of fear and pity[35] – in the audience within a setting which, being distant from the direct personal concerns of the spectators, permitted them to not only experience the emotions safely but to thereby reconceptualise their relation to the role these emotions had in their own lives – to gain pleasurable relief. References to the release of painful emotion through artistic endeavour are to be found elsewhere in Greek literature, and perhaps aid us in interpreting the uncertainties surrounding Aristotle's surviving text. Heath (1996, p.xlii) for example notes Gorgias' description of poetry as arousing "fearful shuddering, tearful pity and a yearning that is fond of grief." Bringing into awareness latent painful emotion and then creating a safe theatre for its release is a feature of much psychotherapeutic and counselling practice. In this lies an important distinction: between emotion that has been stored from an earlier painful experience, and its later release – the act of emotional discharge which occurs under specified conditions, whereby one may be freed from its debilitating effects. Storage and release of emotion are thus the two sides of the cathartic coin. Since Aristotle speaks first of tragedy as a vehicle for arousing latent emotions, prior to his brief reference to their purification, one can infer that he too is aware of the distinction.

That there are these two distinct contexts in which emotions are felt, has led to considerable confusion, not least because of strong public prohibitions (in all cultures) as well as specific gender codes, as to how it is considered acceptable to display different emotions. Well-meaning attempts to curtail distress by interrupting the flow of emotional discharge stem from a basic failure to distinguish between these two contexts. Interrupting emotional discharge, rather than ending distress, only curtails its public display and perpetuates suffering by contributing to its continued storage. The seeming paradox of emotional release, that painful feelings in the course of being re-experienced as they are released produces a pleasurable effect (the relief of tension) is thus not a paradox at all. Aristotle's text can be read as a formal examination of the theatre's enduring capacity to move an audience psychologically. He leaves open the question as to whether this is a matter of design or has been arrived at intuitively – the same question that pervades contemporary debate on psychotherapy as art or science. Whether the practice is one of art or *teknê*, Aristotle's remarks in the *Poetics* should be read as a significant historical landmark in the aesthetics of personal transformation – equal in rank to the Oracle at Delphi, and the temples of Asclepius: a triumvirate of self-purification, self-knowledge and divine dream interpretation. Catharsis, self-knowledge and the meaning of dreams constitute the bedrock upon which Freud built psychotherapy.

When we put Aristotle's text under the lens of contemporary sensibilities one cannot fail to be struck by the narrow range of emotional suffering addressed by it. As suggested above, he sees the mimetic function of tragic theatre as transcending and purifying the pity and fear aroused in it. But what of other painful emotion such as sadness and anger? Aristotle was certainly aware of a greater range of painful emotion – grief and sadness for example were extensively discussed by him in other works – not so in the *Poetics*. How though are we to make sense of the limited "emotional range" of Aristotle's treatise? Whilst he did not share Plato's suspicion of emotions in themselves, there is no doubt that his view regarding the proper expression of them is strongly tied to social norms. This is implicit in the content of Greek tragedy, where the principal characters whose exploits are depicted on the stage, as well as the audience itself, are inevitably of a higher social standing. The characters are in a major way there to remind the audience of the boundaries of right and wrong. Aristotle thereby posits a close relationship between emotion and virtue and with this contends that there is a right way to express emotion – it must find an outlet only in the right circumstances and only to a degree that is acceptable.

One way in which it is acceptable is where the underlying causes of its expression are transparent. Where they are not, they are deemed outside of reason (see for example Horwitz & Wakefield, 2007). This of course is the mistaken basis for modern psychiatry's classification of endogenous and exogenous depression. Unable to interrogate the social norms of emotional expression in Greek society, Aristotle's hands are tied. He lambasts comedy for example: "the laughable is a species of what is disgraceful" which "does not involve pain or destruction" (Aristotle, 1996, p.8). It is a separate species to tragedy, concerned with "an imitation of inferior people" (ibid). Such a view precludes the possibility of embracing comedy as a means for dealing with anger at injustice and therefore laughter cannot be conjoined to the release of tension engendered by injustice. The distinction, at a stroke, both denies the universal psychological benefits of laughter while affirming the rights of Greek elites to be free from lampoon and ridicule.

Since Aristotle, possibilities for challenging the "fossilisation of affect" have varied from the avowedly social to the purely individual. So that while psychotherapy, considered the principle avenue for tackling our emotional ills, might still offer the prospect of liberation from individual distress – talking having almost entirely supplanted feeling and the re-experiencing of feelings, actions and thoughts as the major route to it – the socio-political fabric of life is exempt from an emotional and *public* reckoning. Such a scrutiny remains within the province of dramatic art. But in times of high political drama and tension this is barely sufficient, leaving the truths of public life – and following Boym, the possible and actual freedoms flowing from these – impoverished and the redemptive possibilities of desirable forms of social (re)organisation neglected. The aftermath of the British General Election of 2015 provides a case in point.

With results confounding the expectations of opinion pollsters, the electorate returned a Conservative government promising to abolish the Human Rights Act, further privatise healthcare, social services and education, and continue, under the guise of austerity, an unbridled financial attack on poor and disabled people. The climate within which the election campaign was fought was vicious with undisguised nationalist and racist discourse to the fore. In the wake of this, leading politicians from the defeated Labour Party were asked whether they thought the public had got it wrong. Like rabbits caught in the headlights they chose to confess to their own wrongdoing and further their own demise. Political legitimacy through the ballet box had been interpreted as moral legitimacy; the election moreover mistaken for a purely rational event. Little evidently has been learnt from twentieth-century politics. The sentiment of the wider public, expressing through their vote a desire to make the lives of numerous people more miserable, was considered by legions of political commentators to be both literally and figuratively beyond question or reproach. There was no questioning of the public collective emotional desire to wage a psychological and economic war on vulnerable sections of the populace.

The approaches that both Reich (1975) and Goldhagen (1996) in their different ways offered to account for the German mass psychology of the Nazi period at least began from the stance that a population endorsing human destruction warranted critical interrogation. That the fossilisation of affect, bigotry and cruelty which has evolved alongside the neoliberal order continues to be contained in a political and psychological universe scarcely amenable to public criticism, let alone imagined intervention, is seriously disturbing. In the 1960s and 1970s of the West, the personal became political. In the early twenty-first century it once again became non-political. Though ethics and politics are deeply intertwined, the absence of any desire amongst the political class to address the nature of those connections opens up a dangerous chasm. During the Bosnian crisis of the 1990s, Christopher Hitchens spoke of the British government having reduced the moral temperature to absolute zero. At the present moment it is scarcely any warmer.

Catharsis

In the history of psychoanalysis, the idea of catharsis as a means to heal psychic wounds was first proposed by Freud's colleague Joseph Breuer. It was a "discovery" that Freud insisted remained "the foundation of psychoanalytic therapy" (Freud, 2012, p.237). Breuer had been working with Bertha Pappenheim ("Anna O") who had presented with a diverse assortment of complaints which included limb paralysis, anaesthesia, amnesia, anxiety, hallucinations and disturbances of vision and speech – quite a collection! In their "Preliminary Statement" to *Studies on Hysteria*, Freud and Breuer describe the method they employed. It was, they suggested, successful in removing hysterical symptoms, if they were able to reawaken "the memory precipitating event with complete clarity, arousing with it the accompanying affect, and if the patient then depicted the event in the greatest possible detail and put words to the affect. Remembering without affect almost always fails to be effective" (2004, p.10).

That their famed patient described what they did as "the talking cure" is perhaps unfortunate. Talking appeared to be far from the most important aspect of the cathartic method.

Whether a memory fades or rids itself of affect depends on several factors. Of the greatest importance is whether or not there was an energetic reaction to the affecting event. *By reaction we mean here the whole set of voluntary and involuntary reflexes – from tears to acts of revenge – into which as experience shows, emotions are discharged. If this reaction ensues to a sufficient extent, a large part of the affect will disappear [...] if the affect is suppressed the affect remains bound up with the memory.* (Ibid, p.11, emphasis in original)

It is clear from what they observed that the role of talking was of importance but only in so far as it could either carry the patient's narrative to the memorial source containing the charged affect or carry the affect to be "abreacted," in such a way that the discourse was imbued with passion. Words ("a confession"), deeds ("letting off steam") and tears ("to cry one's eyes out") were the principal means they saw for freeing the disturbing memories of affect. To these they added the effects resulting from "putting the facts right, by considering one's worth" (ibid, p.12) – what in effect amount to verbal contradiction of negative beliefs about the self that were contained within the network of memories being elucidated. These short passages lay bare the foundations upon which psychoanalysis was built. Were Pappenheim still alive today, she would have no doubt been on the receiving end of something pharmacological and different. Initially Breuer and Freud used hypnosis as the means to prize open the memorial contents. Freud later chose to dispense with it, employing at first physical means (head pressure) to awaken dormant memories and later free association to arrive at "the source" by stealth.

Throughout the *Studies on Hysteria*, Breuer and Freud argue that they employ the cathartic method with considerable thoroughness,[36] systematically exploring each element of a set of elicited memories until they are completely drained of emotional charge. In this they describe being initially guided more by the patients' own intuitive self-direction than by any theoretical understanding. Despite the heady endorsements that open the book, in building the foundations of psychoanalysis, Freud came to place less and less emphasis on catharsis and more on his own theoretical speculations concerning the conflicted relationship between conscious and unconscious thought and the defensive and symbolic pathways that link these two together. With Breuer firmly of the opinion that a person's continued difficulties lay in their not having properly dealt with the emotional source of their troubles, they parted company. Breuer's position implied further use and refinement of the method; Freud however did not share his colleague's confidence and for him achieving insight became the primary therapeutic goal – an insight that would be achieved through painstaking psychotherapeutic work and not through the discharge of emotion. Whose insight Freud had in mind – the patient's or the therapist's – is not always apparent.

Thus from kick-starting psychoanalysis and being hailed by Freud as a "momentous discovery" (1990, p.9), producing "deep insight" into the causes of psychological disturbance that could "clear [...] away for ever" chronic hysterical symptoms (Freud & Breuer, 2004, p.20), catharsis moved from the foreground to the background of psychological care. Its importance was relegated to a footnote in the numerous compendiums of abnormal psychology, psychiatry, counselling and psychotherapy. When and why this shift occurred is of some importance, but perhaps an equally important question to be asked about this history is why so many in the psychoanalytic fraternity took at face value Freud's subsequent word that the cathartic method was not in fact effective.

Like Scheff (2001), I am of the opinion that Freud's decision to abandon the centrality of catharsis was a profound mistake. Freud, after all, never gave any convincing reason for having done so. His subsequent abandonment of the so-called "seduction" theory (for which read sexual assault theory) of psychical trauma can equally be considered a less-than-convincing intellectual transformation. Freud replaced his patients' accounts of actual unwanted sexual assaults – in his view "the fundamental precondition for hysteria" (cited in Masson, 1992, p.280) – with explanations couched in terms of a hypothetical constitutional disposition toward producing unconscious fantasies of desired sexual conduct by others (chiefly fathers and uncles) toward them. Freud's published reasons for doing this amount to a series of objections to his seduction theory which he had already effectively dismissed in his original paper on the aetiology of hysteria. That essay contained numerous arguments supporting the credibility of his patients' accounts, which he believed contained both the "relevant suitability to serve as a determinant" and the necessary "traumatic force" (1896, p.262). In addition there were the added factors of the uniformity of these accounts; the significance of the descriptions that the patients gave but that clearly they did not understand; the relationship of the infantile scenes to the context of the entire case history; and the corroborating evidence, in some instances, from third parties. He wrote: "the behaviour of patients while they are reproducing these infantile experiences is in every respect incompatible with the assumption that the scenes are anything else than a reality which is being felt with distress and reproduced with the greatest reluctance" (ibid, p.272).

Masson's (1992) contention that Freud's volte face was a conscious and deliberate attempt to protect psychoanalysis from the intense hostility of a prurient establishment is not easily dismissed – though many in the analytic community have sought to do so. His private correspondence, which Masson's work in the Freud archives revealed, provides ample evidence of this. Freud described himself as "isolated" (cited in Masson, 1992, p.10), "despised and intellectually shunned" (ibid, p.134) when he first presented his account of sexual abuse as the primary causal factor in hysteria. Not entirely unrelated to this were the difficulties initially encountered in trying to earn a living from psychoanalysis. If he maintained that hysteria was a consequence of sexual assault in childhood, then there is little doubt that his professional reputation would have suffered. Smail (2005) believes that this practical problem of securing an income warrants as much consideration as the alleged failure of moral courage that Masson asserts. If these arguments are correct, Freud's dilemma was probably how to stay firm in his conviction that sexual abuse was widespread and a significant factor in the aetiology of psychological disturbance, while requiring the abusers to foot the bill. Not quite a case of the unstoppable force meets the immovable object – but in politics money very often is the immovable object. There was the further issue of Freud's close relationship with Wilhelm Fleiss. Fleiss concocted a number of bizarre theories – the existence of a fundamental biological relationship between the nose and genitals being just one of them. Freud's relationship to Fleiss led him to permit the latter to operate on one of his patients, Emma Eckstein, in an attempt to cure her hysteria. The operation was botched, endangering Eckstein's life. Rather than confront the reality of his folly and Fleiss's incompetence, Freud came to blame the subsequent haemorrhaging on Eckstein's intransigent hysteria. The net result of these combined influences was that psychoanalysis turned away from the real world, and came to adopt a modus operandi of attributing primary causal influences to internal fantasy rather than external traumatic events.

Unsurprisingly, while many in the non-psychoanalytic world greeted Masson's work with sympathy and support, the analytic establishment responded by closing ranks, attacking Masson's character – displaying a prurient interest in his sexual history in their critical reviews or simply ignoring the thrust of Masson's case. Esterson (1998) for example published a lengthy and unconvincing rebuttal, arguing that Freud's methodology and reasoning – in first proposing the seduction theory and later rejecting it – were both suspect. This fails to deal with Masson's point that the psychoanalytic (and wider) establishment were in denial about the evident widespread and familial nature of child sexual abuse. Masson's repeated retort that critical discussants of his work (e.g. Crews, 1996; Porter, 1996) seem incapable of addressing the pervasive extent of sexual abuse in this or any other day does seem warranted. Even Juliet Mitchell, author of *Feminism and Psychoanalysis* (2000), could find no space to mention the controversy when writing the new introduction for her book. Her "radical reassessment of Freudian psychoanalysis" is the poorer for it.

It is of great relevance that Freud's one-time colleague Sandar

Ferenczi was ostracised when he tried to resurrect the seduction theory. Masson contends that a viable alternative psychoanalysis rooted in reality rather than fantasy and favouring the defence of the abused was abandoned along with the seduction theory. The psychiatric historian Roy Porter laments the fact that in the wake of the criticisms of Masson, an opportunity has been missed, for "serious examination [...] of what was lost from explorations of the psyche as a result of Freud's growing and overpowering urge to explain the economy of human consciousness and behaviour in terms of inner, indeed infantile events" (1996, p.289). He considered, no doubt to the chagrin of those who defend Freud, that Masson's work was at least a "halting step forward." Masson's research and its subsequent reception call our attention to a much wider issue. This is the extent to which writers allied to particular institutional practices are really capable of engaging in critical reflection about the ethics of these practices. As academic and professional practice in numerous domains exhibit a slavish adherence to market fundamentalism and the greatness of money, a broad epistemological crisis is taking root. To the extent that genuine critical reflection lies beyond the competence of those institutional actors (individuals and organisations alike) responsible for the dissemination of knowledge, truth has become an economically inaccessible hostage to fortune and the university rather than being a source of intellectual liberation, now stands in danger of becoming an epistemological dungeon.

It is my contention here that one of the things lost was the value of catharsis in personal change. Given what has been said above, one might reflect on whether the future of catharsis as a vehicle for arriving at and unravelling unpleasant truths was in fact tied to the fate of the seduction theory. With Freud's professional reputation at stake one might see it as a case of *catharsis interruptus*. The confrontation between Freud's observations and the market power of conventional morality decided the outcome. It is certainly true that with the emphasis on catharsis, the truth of the patients' utterances occupies a pivotal position in the therapeutic duet. On the other hand, when the patients' tales of the sexual misconduct of others are transformed into fantasy, the case for why such powerful and painful affects should be associated with them – and why, under hypnosis, fantasy rather than reality should be revealed – is far from compelling. As Freud initially argued, the brand of unhappiness he observed first-hand as stemming from an intimate assault provides a very convincing narrative; less so the fanciful and empirically unsupported notion of an unfulfilled fantasy to which the observed suffering was purportedly linked only by virtue of navigating a tortuous theoretical labyrinth. While evidence in any discipline always requires interpretation, the interpretations by themselves are not evidence, a fact that has not always been appreciated by analysts!

Although the demise of catharsis probably owes much to the pressure on Freud to abandon his radical views on the causation of hysteria, there were other factors also at work. A closer reading of Freud and Breuer's entry into psychoanalysis reveals the presence from the outset of a series of assumptions underpinning their method that might have served to further muddy the relevant theoretical (and practical) waters in which they swam. First of all is the presumption that the basic traumatic memories underlying the hysterical phenomena had been completely occluded from consciousness; secondly, that they had found their way into the unconscious by means of repression; thirdly, that the nature of the material needing to be repressed speaks of a conflict within the patient; and fourthly, that talking is the most important means for working through the painful material once access to it has been granted by hypnotic induction. As the basis for a general theory of psychological disturbance, all these ideas are open to challenge. Though the revelations of unconscious motivation were ground-breaking in Freud's day, we can easily forget what his proposals, taken at face value, actually imply, which is that unpleasant events of which a person remains conscious exert no serious debilitating effects on the psyche. Whilst this is compatible with his view that traumas cease to be traumatic once they have made their way into consciousness, it is naïve and scarcely defensible. Nowhere does Freud consider the possibility that hypnosis did nothing more than, on occasion, permit his patients to circumvent strong social customs and speak in a less inhibited manner of things of which they were at least sometimes perfectly conscious, allowing them to do so without the accompanying stigma of responsibility for speaking candidly about what pained them.

The second assumption, though debateable, retains a degree of credibility – though its importance is necessarily restricted to those instances where forgetting has occurred. The third, which situates the warring parties solely within the interiority of the psyche, is also contentious, ignoring the obvious external social dimensions to conflict, which anyway must first occur acted out between people in the real world prior to any hypothetical process of internalisation.

It is the last of these assumptions however, giving primacy to the spoken word, that has exerted the longest-lasting influence on psychotherapy. Despite documenting and highlighting the importance of emotional discharge, Freud and Breuer, on close inspection, appear to have failed to appreciate its real significance. Freud for example describes "shaking and palpitations" as a "mild hysterical attack" (Freud & Breuer, 2004, p.222) – and in the case of Fraulein Elizabeth von R, her crying ("deferred tears") following a bereavement as an act of hysterical reproduction (pp.166-7). These would be understood by many (e.g. Jackins, 1997; Scheff, 2001; Kaufmann & New, 2004) as manifestations not of hysteria but of the discharge of fear and grief. Again, Breuer remarks that sobbing and yelling – responses we would think of as central to the notion of catharsis – "serve no purpose at all" beyond evening out an excess of "cerebral excitation" (Freud & Breuer, 2004, p.204). He seems to understand cathartic action as that which may change an *external* situation rather than bring about *internal* cognitive reappraisal (and accompanying biological readjustment). Neither man appeared interested in developing psychological understanding of affect. Their thinking remains caught in a metaphorical trap in which affective problems are simply a consequence of their abnormal manifest quantity and direction of flow. Their concept of emotion was anchored in the Newtonian physics of the day – caught in the mechanistic crossfire between a system of hydraulic leverage and the accumulation and discharge of static electricity. The opportunity to link the content and meaning of thought with changes in bodily states and emotional regulation thus went begging. Janov (2003), whose work on the effects of early trauma we shall discuss later, was not one to miss this opportunity.

Throughout his collaboration with Breuer, Freud's preferred turn of phrase is to speak of "cathartic analyses" (Freud & Breuer, 2004, p.302) rather than "catharsis" per se, and in fact he makes very few references to the discharge of emotion despite the opening remarks in the "Preliminary Statement." There is much to suggest that he is already intellectually preoccupied with analysing his patients' verbal production and uncovering the hidden history of their thought to the detriment of fully appreciating the therapeutic role of emotional discharge. Analytic thought trumped emotional expression. The Western heritage of splitting thought from emotion – to which Freud has done much to draw our attention – is paradoxically evident from the beginning in his own work.

Freud's disagreements with Breuer regarding the outcome of the treatment of "Anna O" suggest a lack of belief in the method. Though Bertha Pappenheim went on to achieve eminence as a pioneering writer, feminist and social worker, the rise in her fortunes did not follow immediately upon her therapy and Freud considered the cures produced by the cathartic method to be impermanent. He believed the method relieved symptoms rather than dealt with causes and concluded that the most one could hope for from psychoanalysis was deliverance from "hysterical misery into common unhappiness" (ibid, p.306). Furthermore, psychical mechanisms, he declared, played no part in neurasthenia, anxiety neuroses and phobias, and accordingly he believed catharsis was of little value when treating them. No convincing evidential basis is provided for the claim, nor was Freud consistent in upholding this view.

After the *Studies on Hysteria* were published, wish fulfilment, unconscious fantasy and transference entered the therapeutic theatre with force. But, as with his dismissal of catharsis, neither wish fulfilment nor unconscious fantasy were empirically well-supported. In Freud's masterpiece *The Interpretation of Dreams* (1983), for example, although wish fulfilment is hypothesised as the underlying motivational basis for all dreams, one can find nowhere in the lengthy volume an actual example in which the manifest contents of a dream are traced back, via free association, to an unconscious wish. Freud was an assiduous observer and collected vast quantities of data but this curious omission does suggest that in his desire to promote theory he played fast and loose with the kind of empirical facts that would be necessary to support them. In Freud's later reflections on his work, he continued to stress the importance of catharsis, but what really interested him was the outcome of what both the hypnotic method and catharsis purportedly enabled – the fact of making the unconscious conscious. Freud writes:

> *The assertion that the symptoms disappear when one has made their unconscious connections conscious, has been borne out by all subsequent research [...] Our therapy does its work by means of changing the unconscious into the conscious and it is effective only in so far as it has the opportunity of bringing about this transformation.* (2012, p.237)

Freud thus chose to ignore the profound observations regarding the displays of affect he had earlier trumpeted and instead championed insight as the principal therapeutic goal. But did this produce anything better than the transformation of hysterical misery into common unhappiness? Freud's espousal of the merits of psychoanalytic therapy subsequent to his work with Breuer does not suggest that its application produced anything superior to the impermanent cures he attributed to catharsis. Catharsis became the road less travelled and the well-trodden path, an over-intellectualisation – or perhaps it would be better to say over-rationalisation – of the psychotherapeutic encounter. Freud was honest enough to admit that his approach required patients who possessed a "certain level of intelligence" (Freud & Breuer, 2004, p.267). But it is also relevant that he considered his patients' trust and confidence as necessary for the work to be effective – that the "personal relationship with the doctor [...] might even be the sole condition under which the problem can be solved." If that was what he truly believed then perhaps that is the greatest clue as to why the cathartic method was left behind. Freud believed in himself more than he believed in any technique, least of all a technique discovered by somebody else and arguably improperly applied by them both. Charcot pioneered the hypnotic method, Breuer the cathartic method. If Freud persisted with either then his contributions might have been seen as secondary. Where he could make his name was with theory, and his work with Breuer certainly gave him a wealth of new data from which to construct a revolutionary picture of the mind and its operations.

In reviewing the beginnings of psychoanalysis we are confronted with a tale of missed opportunities – of how a different kind of psychoanalysis might have emerged, one that was more comfortable with emotion than words, one that recognised the difference between emotional tension and emotional release, and one that was able to appreciate, practically, the role of the body in the theatre of emotions. This has had far-reaching effects not only on the relationship between academic psychology and psychotherapy and the wider public's understanding of psychotherapy, but also on the development of a good deal of twentieth-century thought.

Catharsis Revisited

1. The Body Politic

It fell to Wilhelm Reich to pick up the baton from where Freud had – not inadvertently – dropped it. Though initially immensely attracted to Freud's ideas on sexuality, libido and emotion, seeing in them confirmation of his own interests in vitalism and mechanistic science, Reich later came to feel an acute sense of disappointment with both Freud and the psychoanalytic movement. From being groomed as Freud's heir apparent, Reich travelled from the analytic inner sanctum to the outer limits and eventual expulsion. His contribution to psychotherapy centred on his concept of body armour whereby the repressive and authoritarian forces of society became physically woven into habitual patterns of neuromuscular tension and activation. These patterns of physical tension, expressing an amalgam of reactionary social ideas and unexpressed emotion, created not merely a rigid and reactionary personality but a veritable obstacle course in the way of vibrant everyday living. This is what Reich referred to as "vegetative streaming," encasing the hapless individual in a fear of freedom and responsibility which was ripe for authoritarian political exploitation and the reproduction of social misery. For Reich the maintenance of the "ordinary marvellous" constituted a principle for his vision of psychology – to be built around an edifice of love, work and knowledge freed from the bounds of social, economic and individual repression. For him, as for Arendt, Benjamin, Baudelaire and Boym, maintaining a sense of wonder in living was a deeply political issue.

Anticipating Foucault in recognising the body as a political conflict zone, Reich's reciprocal mapping of the body politic and the political (human) body is ingenious. In it, sexual repression and economic oppression are destructive bedfellows inextricably bound together. His activism in pre-war Germany advocating sexual-political emancipation, sex education, contraception and abortion went hand in hand with his psychoanalytic work. Unfortunately for Reich, neither the Communist Party on the one hand, nor the psychoanalytic movement on the other, saw psychoanalysis and politics as a marriage made in heaven. He was expelled from both, leaving only Eric Fromm ten years later and Ronnie Laing another twenty beyond that to build theoretical bridges between psychotherapy and Marxism. Though the concept of catharsis received little or no theoretical elaboration from Reich it was central to his practice and has remained influential in the various therapeutic offshoots from his work – body psychotherapy, gestalt, the Alexander technique and primal therapy to name but a few.

In terms of contemporary psychotherapeutic practice a case can be made that Reich's influence is on a par with Freud's. So how did catharsis figure in Reichian therapy? Reich's biographer Myron Sharaf describes one such session:

I was extremely impressed by the way Reich worked with my body. He would have me breath and then keep pointing out the way I avoided letting the breath expire naturally. Sometimes, he would press certain parts of my body, particularly my chest. A few times, this was followed by very deep sobbing, crying in a way I could not remember ever having cried before. He would encourage me in an empathic way: 'Don't be ashamed of it. I have heard it by the millions. That sorrow is the best thing in you.' (Sharaf, 1994, p.24)

Reich then would intervene directly and physically to dismantle a patient's muscular armour. The jaw, neck, chest, abdomen or thighs for example were areas of the body where intervention might be more likely to produce outpourings of crying, rage or laughter and on occasion recovery of occluded memories. Reich linked the changes in muscular tension to specific changes in autonomic function when emotional arousal was stimulated. This key feature of his analysis meant that he was distinguishing between emotional distresses (e.g. fear, grief) and emotional expression (e.g. laughter, shaking, crying) which signal a healing response to the distress. This was a very different kind of psychoanalysis to Freud's, with the royal road to the unconscious being not dream interpretation but bodily manipulation. The guardians of the unconscious – the defence mechanisms guarding the psyche – were not disembodied mental entities or the intrapsychic operations (projection, introjection, denial, repression, splitting, etc.) as envisaged by Freud, but primarily physical bodily structures and processes which had come to assume an habitual form. When these patterns were disrupted, a free-flowing catharsis ensued, simultaneously restoring a sense of vibrancy, alertness and aliveness with accompanying relaxing changes in posture, facial expression and breathing. This has an intriguing parallel with Vygotsky's[37] somewhat original take on catharsis as resulting from an affective contradiction, "an antagonism between form and content" (Boym, 2010, p.54) in a work of art. Body therapy (vegetotherapy[38]) was Reich's dynamic work of art, with the muscular armour constituting the form. Only when this armour is directly contradicted by physical work are the emotional and mental contents previously held in place revealed. Vygotsky's proposal that this catharsis "slows down violent emotion,"[39] as Boym says, "transforming it into a form of emotional wisdom, play, tolerance and pleasure" (ibid, p.55) could have come straight out of Reich's own publications.

Like Freud's early forays into catharsis, Reich's work contains a distinct rejection of the Western regard for emotions as irrational or illogical. Far from being irrational, the emotional expression in catharsis, along with its corresponding changes induced at the cognitive, behavioural, anatomical and physiological levels, heralds a disintegration of irrationality, a disruption of "habituated perception" (Paterson, 2005, p.164) and a return to a physically grounded rationality. Reich's work also represents one of psychology's more innovative attempts to look beyond its borders and get to grips with the relationship between the individual and the social as well as integrate the cognitive, behavioural and emotional. However, like Freud, Reich was bewitched by the scientific paradigms inherited from Newtonian mechanics. Freud laboured under the belief that his psychological concepts had to be reformulated in a language of biological drives, impulses and energies, whilst Reich underpinned his sexual-politics, psychotherapy and body work in terms of its relationship to the orgone, a new form of cosmic energy that he believed he had discovered. It was to be Reich's undoing. In the opening to Makavejev's cinematic homily to Reich, *WR: Mysteries of the Organism*, we are invited, in successive screenshots, to "enjoy, feel, laugh." The guardians of officialdom did none of these things.

Reich's attempts to harness orgone energy for the improvement of human health and to combat what he saw as the devastating environmental effects of nuclear testing were met with scepticism and legal force on the part of the authorities who ordered him to stop distribution of the Orgone Energy Accumulators he was making. Reich claimed that the devices, variations on the Faraday cage, were able to concentrate orgone energy. His refusal to comply with the Food and Drug Administration's orders set in motion a chain of events leading to his imprisonment, the banning of his books, the destruction of the devices, and an end to his UFO-watching and experiments in controlling the weather. Just as his attacks on his patients' character armour had brought forth tears, his cloudbusters summoned tears of rain from the heavens – at least that was what was claimed. The evidence for their efficacy, though not compelling, is intriguing, but with his imprisonment they were to do so no more. Reich died in a Federal Penitentiary, having lived long enough to enjoy the dubious distinction of having his books burned by both the US and Nazi governments. Hailed as a visionary by some and a crank by others – and despite his influence on psychotherapy and his pioneering of sexual politics – he remains a tragic figure, cast drift on the fringes of the humanities, and unheard of by today's armies of psychology students. Reich believed he was a man of the future. What he would have made of today's environmental awareness, the preoccupation with human-induced climate change, to say nothing of the greater cultural familiarity with Eastern notions of qi or ki – a universal free-flowing energy permeating reality – is anybody's guess. He attributed his own persecution to the fear and emotional plague endemic in the wider society. No doubt, in the dangerous power wielded by today's transnational corporations, in their alliance with media and government, and in the concomitant acquiescent mass psychology that follows from this unholy trinity, he would recognise the same emotional plague that had stricken his contemporaries. "They do it only because life has escaped them," he wrote (1974, p.127).

2. *Early Life, Transformation and Redemption*
The expulsion of catharsis from the centre stage of psychotherapy is a distinctly modern phenomenon, illustrating perhaps a distinctly modern discomfort with our emotions. Nowhere is this more evident that at the heart of cognitive psychology, which in its quest to produce a simulacrum of human intelligence appears oblivious to emotion's presence. This is an attempt to avoid the age-old problems of the human condition by ignoring the very condition of being human at any age. Cognitive psychology in its disembodied incarnation is thus incapable of a critique of itself or of where we stand on the broader stage, capable only of cranking

up the speed on the experimental train ride to existential oblivion. This leaves us with a vision of humanity that has not so much been polished in order to present us in a better light – a "varnishing of reality" (Boym, 1995, p.109) – but has been polished to present us in no light whatsoever: what one might refer to as a vanishing of reality.

Attempts in the healing arts to redress human suffering through a cleansing of emotion did not end with Reich. In the early 1970s primal therapy was proposed by Janov as a means of freeing people from the consequences of early childhood pain. His ideas have much in common with the central tenets of co-counselling: that healing requires connecting to and re-experiencing early childhood distress with full conscious awareness of the context in which it first arose. In a poetical and seemingly paradoxical invocation of Marx, Janov declared that "he who does not relive the past is doomed to repeat it" (2003, p. 346). The reliving, however, is neither tragic nor farcical, but comprises a process of recovery which is lengthy and which requires recent pains to be integrated prior to any progression to earlier, more damaging and imprinted hurts. The accompanying re-evaluation and re-integration is both psychological – the outward catharsis of emotion is a core feature of the process – and physiological, as memory of past trauma is written into the body as much as it is the mind. Considerable skill on the part of the therapist is needed to engender the necessary safety for the healing process to run its natural course and for clients to open themselves to feeling deeply painful experiences once more. Though Janov writes that "a therapy without tears [...] in effect can never be effective" (ibid, p.xxiv), what he really has in mind is the whole panoply of emotional expression: laughter, rage, trembling as well as crying.

When we reflect on what is traditionally meant by stress or distress, writers usually speak of a mismatch between one's current resources and the demands placed on them. Such a defin-ition, though not without merit, is unsatisfactory for a number of reasons, not the least of which is that it implies a somewhat mechanistic process at work and avoids any consideration of the actual content of distress. Janov's answer to this is that what is present in all such early trauma – indeed in most trauma – is the recorded feeling of not being sufficiently loved. As with Reich, for Janov too, love goes to the heart of the human mystery and in primal therapy is seen as fundamental to the fulfilment and satisfaction of all human needs whatever the developmental level. This also implies that distresses that arise as a result of accident – for example being in a car crash – are less emotionally damaging than those which arise as a consequence of the activities of human actors with whom one is already emotionally connected and from whom one expects loving attention and care.

A further distinction of interest in Janov's work, and one that his critics have not fully appreciated, concerns the dramatising and acting-out of emotion (what Janov perhaps unhelpfully terms "abreaction") in the hope of gaining access to underlying feelings. This dramatising stands in contrast to the deepest and most uninhibited expression of painful feelings through catharsis. Healing without suffering is thus not possible. Not surprisingly Janov's work has been much maligned, criticised as lacking scientific rigour and said to possess little evidence in its favour. The same, of course, could equally be said of much psychotherapy. The real problem in any assessment of primal therapy – of which Janov himself was acutely aware – concerns the nature of what is delivered in the therapy, to say nothing of what is being evaluated and how. Much of what has been offered in the name of primal therapy has been disowned by Janov himself, precisely because of the failure to differentiate between dramatised emotion and the real cathartic expression of long-dormant painful feelings. The skill of the therapist is crucial here and similarly any researcher coming to consider a thorough research evaluation of the process must perforce have a clear understanding of what the process actually is. As the academic community continues to have a problematic relationship with emotion, it is probably fair to say that an appropriate and thorough scientific evaluation is still awaited.

3. Estrangement, Catharsis and Change

It has been said that modernity began "with the discovery that the book of the world is written in prose" (Bruns, cited in Shklovsky, 2015, p.ix). In psychotherapy it is Freud, initially at least, who best exemplifies this realisation. But the nature of the prose is all-important and Freud's poetic, discursive assimilation of the art of psychotherapy was soon enough buried beneath the meandering mountain of scientific verbiage that collapsed on top of it. The poetry wasn't all that was buried in the ruins. Shklovsky's art of estrangement was intended to dismember the stultifying habits that prevent us from addressing reality as it is, from experiencing in thought and feeling what exactly is going on, both the dreadful and the joyous. His distinction between "recognition" and "seeing" is crucial to understanding the practices of estrangement and our own displacement from the possibilities of seeing what stands before us. The word "before," in this case, is alluding to both to what is in front of us spatially and what is behind us temporally. Both are essential ingredients of the experience of "now." Seeing is the dynamic creative injection of awareness into one's perception so that what is flowing into our senses can be fully appreciated. "Automatization," wrote Shklovsky, "eats away at things, at clothes, at furniture, at our wives, and our fear of war" (2015, p.5). In his *Theory of Prose* he examined the various ways in which the automation – we might even say the mechanisation – of experience is estranged by the writer. The evolution and purpose of fiction was not so much to represent reality but to lay bare the usually unconscious devices through which we automatically structure, plot and narrate the human passage through life. Yesterday's inventive device is today's cliché – hence we wage a perpetual struggle against kitsch and the invasion of banality. The arts and the sciences are thereby not merely different but locked in an eternal dialectic: the sciences to reduce the complexity, vibrancy and vitality of the world to schematic formulaic repetition; and the arts to use, where necessary, whatever structure, plot and device is at hand in order to return a sense of vibrancy, fluidity and aliveness to our appraisal of, and presence in, the world. Scientists often pursue the holy grail of discovery drawn by the allure of the new; the artist on the other hand turns away from novelty per se toward a reckoning with the emotional truths of existence. Though each pursues depth of knowledge in different directions, they may on occasion meet in the realm of beauty.

Considered as the art of healing the soul, many of the techniques, practices and strategies used in psychotherapy and counselling may be construed as devices of estrangement, in order to work upon pain a "sea-change into something rich and strange" (Shakespeare, *The Tempest*). "We must," Shklovsky wrote, "extricate a thing from the cluster of associations in which it is bound" (2015, p.60). Is not the core of healing built upon the attempt to see our lives outside of their usual context? For example, the use of facial expression, vocal intonation, verbal, physical and emotional contradiction can serve to dislocate a client from the observational platform erected from their experiences of distress and to substitute for this an entirely new vantage point for viewing reality, self and others (see Kauffman & New, 2005, for further discussion). Similarly, irony and satire, also useful in psychotherapy, have long been recognised as means of speaking to power – not surprising then that in official psychological discourse these are entirely absent and a form of emotionless discourse is taken as a byword for truth, objectivity and value. The "grammar" of artistic rhythm in Shklovsky's view was to systematise the disruptions and disturbances of prose which return colour to the grey world of the text and permit stories to be told, retold, reinvented, embellished, impeded, restructured and disrupted as acts of invention to replace timeworn forms of narrating that have "outlived [...] artistic usefulness" (Shklovsky, 2015, p.20). Are there then equivalent "laws" or strategies, analogous to those of plot formation, that can be applied to the encounters we designate as psychotherapeutic and healing? A literal transplantation of Shklovsky's dissection of plot devices to psychotherapy is problematic – not least because of the myriad forms of psychotherapy. However, the task of delineating an aesthetic of psychotherapy becomes less arduous if we consider the means enacted in any therapeutic encounter that successfully estranges us from the structured diet of unchallenged assumptions and expectations which permeate our unhappiness, as equivalent devices of intent and purpose. *Sentimental Journey*, Shklovsky's (1970/1922) memoir written in the immediacy of the Russian revolution, contains a telling account of the estrangement of battlefield horror and its connection to emotional release. Following an explosion,

> *our soldiers, surrounded by enemies, were waiting for a train to come for them; while waiting, they busied themselves by picking up and putting together the shattered pieces of their comrades' bodies.*
> *They picked up the pieces for a long time.*
> *Naturally some of the pieces got mixed up.*
> *One officer went up to the long row of corpses.*
> *The last body had been put together out of the leftover pieces.*
> *It had the torso of a large man. Someone had added a small head; on the chest were small arms of different sizes, both left.*
> *The officer looked for a rather long time; then he sat on the ground and burst out laughing... laughing... laughing...* (cited in Vatulescu, 2005, p.41)

Shklovsky believed the job of art was to distinguish illusion from reality (Smoliarova, 2005), an undertaking that required not just returning vitality to perception but also to emotional sensation. Is this not the very same challenge that faces the client in psychotherapy? Not to confront reality, defend oneself from it or deny it – but to live at ease in it. The hallmark of both Shklovskian estrangement and co-counselling is the employment of contradiction – often a disjunction between what is said and how it is said – to reveal reality. These contradictions can be consciously designed but as Shklovsky's example indicates they don't have to be. Our distresses remain tied to us precisely because they operate to a large degree implicitly – woven into our habitual modes of living. For human beings, the required restructuring of semantic networks into which we are tied is so often the work of emotions, and emotional expression is invariably triggered when our assumptions about how reality operates are given an unexpected jolt. Thus we need to look toward the estrangement of our problematic emotional habits in any analysis of psychotherapy. The notion of a core self is our most favoured and cherished personal narrative, and our beliefs or disbeliefs about who we are and what we are capable of are the source of either triumph or despair. To return to co-counselling: the general stance of the counsellor directed toward contradicting ingrained distresses is concerned with the provision of confidence, approval, interest, respect, delight, high expectations and love; valuing the integrity and goodness of the other (Jackins, 1997) coupled with an openness and acceptance of their feeling and expressing emotional hurt. Holding these positions toward oneself facilitates the (emotional and cognitive) transformation of self from old to new.

It is of interest that in their examination of the history of estrangement, Holquist and Kliger (2005, p.614) unwittingly expose the common purpose behind both estrangement as artistic practice and psychotherapy. Estrangement for them entails "a view of life grounded in a *division*," such that "a split is perceived within the individual subject between some version of a core self and... *something else.*" The disruption in question is relational in nature rather than a cleavage in some imagined fragmented and static essential self. The intent behind artistic (and psychotherapeutic) estrangement is therefore to heal this rift, to reunite and reconnect the divided self, to move it into a dynamic equilibrium/harmony with the flux of the world. Thus the transformation of the "self" brought about by estrangement is not a transformation wrought on an *isolated* self distinct from the world, which is the paradigmatic icon of Kant's view of human alienation. Rather it is a transformation of our contextual relationships with ourselves in and with the world, amounting to a destabilisation of identity (Rutenburg, 2005), in so far as one's "self" is constructed from a habitual outlook. The "divided self," depicted by both Winnicott and Laing, fundamentally entails a division between a stagnated self, moored in perpetual stasis, and a self that remains alive in an open sea of continual becoming.

There has been much confusion in this area. Post-modernist views of a constructed self call into question notions of an authentic self but as Roberts and Itten (2006) have argued the concept of authenticity can be maintained if, rather than being seen as a measure of faithfulness to oneself, it references a particular mode of being – how one acts in relation to the conjunction of forces that impinge on them.

One can act to resist these forces or act in harmony with them. In the Shaolin practise of pushing hands in martial-arts training, for example, one comes to learn that stronger forces may on occasion be overcome not by a direct meeting of force against force, but through attuning oneself to the flow of energy of one's opponent. As the forces aligned against one reach their zenith, the predominance of Yang may be replaced by Yin and the flow of energy can be harnessed, displaced from oneself or returned towards the opponent. An authentic state of being can be described as attuned to this

natural flow of energy, in, through and around oneself; this is an
engagement with one's whole being, neither purely physical nor
mental – a coherence in which, as Bruce Lee observes, "there is
neither fighter, nor opponent – only the fight." (Roberts & Itten,
2006, p.794)

From this perspective identities are simply fleeting narratives,
neither real nor authored: "a language field in which 'identity' is
less a property of a given character than a fluid state that takes on
various shapes and that hence engages the reader to participate
in its formation and deformation" (Perloff, 1992; cited in
Edmond, 2006, p.102). Emerson (2005, p.637) argues that in
estrangement, distancing trumps identification. This sense of a
recoverable, vital process is what the work of estrangement is
directed towards, keeping open the channels of an optimal
engagement with the world. This work is never complete.
Whichever new context the practice inserts into life is vulnerable
to the same processes of routinisation and automation that
pervade human life. In a therapeutic context what this means is
an active distancing from any identification with one's own
distress. There is no essential self, no internal essence distinct
from the world, but a nature that is inseparable from nature itself.
It is almost as if Shklovsky is anticipating Bruce Lee – gain familiarity with the forms of martial movement in order to cultivate no
form (defamiliarise them). To fight without fighting. To move
with stillness.

Here at the frontier, there are falling leaves.
Although my neighbours are all barbarians,
And you, you are a thousand miles away,
There are always two cups on my table
– Anon (cited in Exley, 1992)

But whatever shall be is a promise only
– Osip Mandelstam (1991, p.86)

Six

The Tao of Estrangement: Martial Art, Psychology and Reality

The enlightened warrior remains open to the signs from all quarters. There is a pattern to things for those who choose to see it
– Peter Hobart (2003, p.107)

The acceptable and the unacceptable are both acceptable
– Lao Tzu (cited in Pao, 2010, p.20)

If it is to emerge from the crisis that envelops it, psychology must be deconstructed and destabilised. Bowman contended, following Derrida, that deconstruction is a martial art, employing the same economies of force and violence – the five-word secret, "listen, stick, yield, neutralise, attack (or sometimes 'control' or 'issue force')" – as are found in Tai Chi (Bowman, 2007, p.5). In physical combat this deconstruction of the other's line of defence is invariably spatial – an acute specialisation within the bounds of psychogeography. The challenge of arriving at or discovering a professionally "method-less" psychology (by which I mean a psychology that does not utilise "professional" methods but that aids people to know and live in the world in a better way than we currently manage) may be likened to the challenge facing the martial artist when confronted with an opponent. The task may be considered in a variety of ways: to disrupt their flow of vital energy (qi); to steal; to misdirect their attention to where they mistakenly believe it will be best placed for their defence; or to simply destabilise habitual patterns of response – estrangement as the art of attack (or defence). Here then we will explore some of the off-modern possibilities for psychology which can be found in the arts of combat by opening up some neglected spaces concerning identity, energy, change, memory, perception, reality and politics.

Bruce Lee famously said that the student must first aspire to learn particular styles, forms and routines of attack and defence (often the two are the same) – the grammar of fighting – in order to play with and ultimately discard them. In some Kung Fu systems these forms have developed from close observation of specific animals (tiger, crane, monkey, praying mantis and snake), signifying an important ecological dimension to defence. Acquisition of form was, for Lee, the prerequisite to inventing one's own way in the world, being an indissoluble part of it, at one with the active defence of self and others. This principle lies at the heart of the Shaolin code of ethics (Ke-Wit, 1981). The Shaolin art is geared toward training the three inner faculties of a person – *Chin, She* and *Qi* – essence, mind-power and intrinsic energy respectively. The result of training is a propensity, a way of being with the world which stands *for* something – the principles for example of right action, harmony, justice and freedom; often symbolised by the bamboo – flexible and yielding, yet strong and firm, solid from the outside yet empty within (Payne, 1997).

That many varieties of martial arts have their roots in Taoist and Buddhist philosophy is no accident. These belief systems are inherently value-laden and political. They stress the transformation of the self as a principle for living in harmony with the world. The maxim of Heraclitus, the "wondrous," "weeping philosopher" – that "you cannot step twice into the same stream" – is congruent with the philosophical underpinnings of Shaolin practice. Like the adepts of Kung Fu, alternating between yin and yang, soft (gentle and supple) and hard (strong as steel) styles, Heraclitus stressed the unity of opposites and the ever-changing nature of reality. Shklovsky's art of estrangement – to continually defamiliarise that which has been turned to perceptual stone – is thus a way to affirm this constant flux of the real.

The roots of Shaolin Kung Fu lie in the development of physical practices intended to strengthen the body and free the mind from worry, spearheaded by the arrival at the Shaolin temple of an Indian Buddhist prince (Da Mo) in 527 AD. Considering the monks to be weak and himself exceedingly patient, Da Mo meditated for nine years on ways to assist them. The result was two books: one geared towards developing the Buddhist spirit (*Shi Sui Ching*); the other to fortifying the physical body (*Yi Gin Shing*). The latter grew into the martial methods now associated with the temple. In the Chinese language "Kung Fu" literally means energy (*kung*) and time (*fu*), thereby denoting in combination the patient accomplishment of skill (Jwing-Ming, 1982). This is a reflective process which in many ways relies upon a form of estrangement from the world. This estrangement is necessary not only to cultivate one's abilities over time but also to observe and reflect on the nature of the world after which one may contend with the forms of dislocation in it. Kung Fu teaches the benign application of force in order to deal (on occasion) with the presence of malevolent or harmful forces (Ke-Wit, 1981). As such it becomes a type of psychological and behavioural knowledge rooted in the everyday. The Buddhist and Taoist philosophy underlying Kung Fu, like that of Heraclitus, embraces a view of reality as impermanent, formless and in flux. With no-thing in the world, there is nothing to hang onto.

Look, it cannot be seen – it is beyond form.
Listen, it cannot be heard – it is beyond sound.
Grasp, it cannot be held – it is intangible.
These three are indefinable, they are one. (Lao Tzu, cited in Pao, 2010, p.45)

"Sages have no fixed mind" (Chuang-Tzu, 1993, p.38). In *The Human Condition* Arendt writes in strikingly similar terms of "the over-all gigantic circle of nature itself, where no beginning and no end exist and where all natural things swing in changeless, deathless repetition" (1998, p.96)... a world "into which single individuals, unique, unexchangeable and unrepeatable entitles, appear and from which they depart" (ibid, p.97). But while we may consider the world of things and the self as illusion,[40] our relationships with others lie at the centre of the reality we must contend with. Psychology as art, estranged and off-modern, with multiple de-centred axes of orientation, embraces the principle of paradox. One cannot learn self-defence – without doubt a paradoxical undertaking given the presupposed non-existence of the self – without a solid relationship of trust and respect between persons. This de-centred notion of self has relevance for how we think, not only about personhood but also our relations within the wider society. It challenges not only theorists who propose top-down hierarchical structures of personality as "inherited," but also political scientists and social commentators whose manifest belief in hierarchical political governance and "strong" leadership has been an unquestioned mantra in how we think about the social and political world. Ideas, as Bowman has proposed, can be as deadly as any strike on a key pressure point.

When I began learning martial arts many people I spoke with were eager to know which "belt" I had. But belts are only for holding up one's trousers. The belt system in martial arts is very recent – first introduced in the late nineteenth century in the then-new martial art of Judo – and is far from ubiquitous. The ranking systems in many schools are not standardised and the awarding of "black" belts has on some occasions owed more to a desire for profit than a wish to reward talented students. It speaks more of our obsession with class and status than the cultivation of spiritual learning and practice. At its worst there are training halls where a student's ability to pay has been ranked ahead of their ability to demonstrate the required skill for a designated rank. These have been referred to somewhat disparagingly as McDojos.[41]

I never learnt any hierarchical system beyond the fact that I was a student learning from a master, one who taught me that he also learnt from me – that each lesson went in both directions – a reality where the roles of teacher and student were one, both terms abstractions from a relationship of mutual learning. Bruce Lee also stressed the human-relational side of training – often with humour. The art of fighting could not be learnt, he said, without fighting. He compared learning martial arts without sparring to learning to swim on dry land (Bolelli, 2008, p.198). But in that characteristic dance with paradoxical logic, Lee also said that the highest form of the art of fighting was not-fighting. In one of those quirks of life, a monument of Lee was unveiled in Mostar, Bosnia and Herzegovina in November 2005, ten years after the end of the Bosnian War. The statue, by Croatian sculptor Ivan Fijolić, was erected in response to the wishes of the Mostar Urban Movement youth group, a nostalgic reference to happier times when the citizens of multi-ethnic Socialist Yugoslavia revelled in the Kung Fu craze of the 1970s and '80s. Lee's statue was chosen by the organisers as a symbol of the fight against ethnic divisions. "Now they can rack their brains trying to decide whether he is Bosniak, Croat or Serb," said one of the youth group (cited in Chong, 2012, p.232). Davis Miller described Lee as a "mover," his body as singing its own song, a "riveting, righteous, sanctifying, purifying" explosion of grace and movement (2000, p.13). The dazzling physical prowess evidenced in his Hollywood debut in 1973 brought many people into martial arts. I was still at school then. Suddenly other kids began coming out of the woodwork proclaiming their devotion to the sacred arts which, if they were to be believed, they had been practising for years. No doubt the youth of Yugoslavia were similarly galvanised and would swap outlandish tales of "chop socky" from Dubrovnik to Belgrade. Lee would no doubt have been pleased that some of his teaching, as well as a sense of humour, survived the bloodshed in the Balkans.

The martial arts embody a different concept of action than that predicated in the subject-verb-object, grammatical carving up of the world. In it, action reveals not simply our presence in the world, as Arendt argued, but the nature of the world as continual transfer of energy. Much, if not all, of what one learns in martial training concerns one's relation to this energy flow. We live in the perpetual streaming now – an amalgam of the near past permeating the anticipated future, according to Bergson (2002). Contemporary neuroscience concurs with this, attributing our sense of flowing continuity to the operations of working memory. The illusion of now, it is argued, is built on a synchronised hierarchical set of brain processes operating over different intervals of time: a general sense of continuity (over thirty seconds); the experienced moment (two to three seconds); and the functional moment (measured in milliseconds and dependent on sensory filtration) (Spinney, 2015).

This has implications for our understanding of time and its *a priori* psychological foundation, the currency of all our experience, *duration*, described by Bergson as "the continuous progress of the past which gnaws into the future" (2002, p.211) and "the very substance of the world" (ibid, p.230). Under an imagined different processing scenario – the elasticity of the time perceived as "now" – the duration of the changing moment could in principle be extended considerably, allowing for the possibility of experiencing the temporal unfolding of a given "linear sequence" of events as occurring in the same moment. The perception of this moment implies not an awareness of stasis, but an enhanced cognisance of the expansion of time, in which one observes the endless advance and retreat of events from the theatre of being; permitting acknowledgement of a unified organic whole within the changing configuration of events.

Contemplating reality as a single undivided and unbroken totality challenges our accepted ideas of free will, causality and determinism; invites us to see these, first and foremost, as human constructions which emerge from within the cognitive horizons of our take on reality. All the elements of this conceptual triad are underpinned by our culturally acquired, now habitual, view of linear time. The experience of yogis, meditators and martial artists notwithstanding, the scientific community, in both physics and psychology, has struggled to engage with the implications that the Bergsonian view of time has for our present understanding of existence. In both disciplines, the nature of consciousness, its relationship to the material world and the enigma of time occupy pivotal positions.

In over thirty years of life in higher education, no element of any syllabus I have been acquainted with has ever given any attention to the enigma of existence. Nor has it had much to say about the human nature of the learning relationship, nor to cultivating specific states of mind or acquiring the means to defend oneself emotionally and physically. No psychologist has yet to seriously question whether the antidote to bullying in schools might not be a form of martial-arts training capable of imbuing young people with discipline, respect and control. Yet improvements in self-esteem, a more positive response to physical challenge, greater autonomy, emotional stability and assertiveness as well as reductions in anxiety and depression have all been associated with martial-arts training (Macarie & Roberts, 2010). Attention has also been drawn to the social benefits of such behavioural change – in particular the relationship between martial-arts practice and aggression (see Konzak & Boudreau, 1984).

Yet we all know in our hearts that we learn best of all from those we like and love and when we also feel loved. That this quality of human relationships – described by poets as the "one common miracle" (Patten, 2007, p.12), which "unbolts the dark" (Thomas, 2000, p.145) – stirs the undercurrents, in all the corners of the world, to all that is good in life is unmistakeable. Yet in Western psychology it remains largely absent, a void filled by an empirical grasping for some tangible biological essence – the Holy Grail and source of human nature. For Arendt, as for Sartre, this reductionist endeavour would be looked upon as fruitless, for "the essence of who somebody is," the totality of a given person's qualities, "can only come into being once life has departed," not before it (Arendt, 1998, p.193). A human life can be "grasped as a palpable entity" only once it has ended. For Laurie Anderson (2015) this moment of transition, the point at which we leave the world, marks the time when death's purpose is known and revealed; the release of love; love and death at the beginning and end of existence.

If the same reasoning were applied to the human species as a whole, then we could agree with Marx that the essence of humanity, as a collective, can only be realised and known historically; however to do so in actuality would require the extinction of the human species – the completion of the biological-species project that is humanity – and the presence of a non-human cognate entity to do the appraising. Perhaps we allow so much hate to fill the world because we cannot see beyond life. Given the obvious difficulties of determining an ahistorical (or trans-historical) human essence, less biologically oriented psychologists have sought refuge in the concept of identity, which, when deconstructed into its constituent personal and social elements and duly reified, has been employed to explain the unsavoury "nature" of human social conflict down through the ages. But there is nothing "essential" in the way we construct identity or the notion that we must construct it at all, or that we must eschew action for contemplation; and nothing inevitable in the fact that identity is routinely constructed in opposition to others. As such it remains a conceptual shrine to the psychological invention of *things* amidst the ceaseless flow and change of the world. Boym notes how "revelation of mortality is of no use for group identity" (2001, p.78). It is arguably the antidote to it. To foresee the inevitability of our own death as a natural process stands at one end of a continuum. At the other end lies the desire to inflict death preternaturally on others.

The transience of the group as well as the transience of physical artifices that pepper human civilisation are facts of life, anathema to the purveyors of invented tradition and restorative nostalgia. Ignoring or denying the ravages and contents of time's works is not however the same as defeating them. Consigning the inconvenient truths of the past to institutional or personal oblivion is never a completely successful undertaking. As Freud so deftly argued, reality sooner or later bites back. The repressed returns. And by the same token, the "revelation" of group identity is of little use for immortality. The national and supranational entities (from the Party to the Volk) whose litany of crimes stains the historical record seldom last very long. Though the storms of these past traumas are carried by the historical tide, Benjamin's angel of history does get its moments of reprieve. The horrors of yesteryear do subside. The present in which we live is different. Everything that rises also fades.

The idea of learning, developing and *becoming* through love and the absence of ego runs through the best and most profound martial disciplines and philosophical traditions, where the idea of identity sits uneasily. Lao Tzu, the author of the *Tao Te Ching*, expressed this most clearly. "When I let go of what I am, I become what I might be" (cited in Pao, 2010, p.39). This is human life as a process, a part of the natural order; a movement from itself toward itself. It is inherently creative, a co-creation between humanity and nature. "Art," Ernst Fischer remarked, "must show the world as changeable, and help to change it" (2010, p.48). A psychology that does not incorporate the principles of development, change and creativity at its heart must be considered a failure.

Buddhist perspectives entered into the Western consciousness during the 1960s and '70s and for a short while suggested a different set of goals for those with an interest in psychology. For a brief interlude Western psychology flirted with its enchanted Eastern counterpart. Robert Ornstein's (1972) book *The Psychology of Consciousness* became a bestseller seeking to woo readers with an intoxicating mixture of Zen, Yoga and fledgling neuroscience. Ornstein's wish was to unite the ways of the "left" and "right" brain into a coordinated exploration of reality. By questioning established notions of causality and linear time, he sought to appeal to the generation whose drug-induced experiments with reality and challenges to the status quo had expanded not merely their consciousness but also their unconscious. The publishers of his book certainly thought so – describing it on the back cover as an area "not normally discussed in psychology courses" (they were right, it certainly wasn't discussed in mine) and "comprehensible to people without a psychology background." Nowadays it would appear almost incomprehensible to people *with* a psychology background! Yet for a brief moment in the illusion of our time, the East fruitfully met with the West and raised the possibility that Enlightenment rationalism might be expanded to embrace an altogether different intellectual and aesthetic sensibility, one less structured by notions of causality, reductionism, linear time and the physical and psychological isolation of material entities.

Its rejection from the mainstream currents of Western psychological thought, however, does not derive from any inherent inevitability in the direction of Western thought nor mean that they cannot be revisited and bloom once more. The nature of the energetic systems theorised as permeating the universe and embodied in the practices of Tai Chi and numerous martial arts are much closer to a physicists' view of reality (Capra, 1984; Zukav, 1984) and suggest knowledge not as a thing but as a way, a path or journey – an adventurous epistemological art. Anderson expressed her accord with this view as follows: "For me Buddhism and being an artist is the same. There are no beliefs connected to either one of them. You don't have to believe anything. All you have to do is pay attention. That's what an artist is" (cited in Felsenthal, 2015).

Nature exists beyond the written but can be danced and sparred with. As the clock runs down on the global assault on the biosphere, the spiritual and defensive potentialities of these practices could yet be added to a refashioned critical eco-modernity, where a rapprochement between intellectual and practical knowledge comes as part of the package. Martial arts, meditation and Zen are ultimately forms of knowledge that attune one to the rhythms of life, as well as preparing one for the inevitability of loss and the concomitant necessity to let go, and which also celebrate "the elemental happiness that comes from being alive" (Arendt, 1998, p.108).

For psychological knowledge, as we usually conceive of it in the West, to function in this way it would need to be de-anchored from any currently organised professional base and end its symbiotic relationship with the capitalist system. To set one's sights in this direction is to accept an invitation to estrange psychology from itself and return it to a place in the everyday familiar world; to participate in a cycle of de-familiarisation and re-familiarisation that is reminiscent of the steps toward the Buddhist goal of individual enlightenment as well as the return home. This is "the place not yet visited, built out of longings, mapped out by accidents" (Patten, 1981, p.43). Then one may finally know the discipline for the first time, and then psychology, having found its way back to life, may finally know itself and dissolve into life.

Though not what we have been led to believe, feeling is intrinsic to knowing the world. Boym resolutely anchors this to the off-modern, an approach that she sees as "a form of passionate thinking engaged in a double movement between theory and practice" (2008, p.37). "Guided by wonder," it dances between the "imaginary" and "material experience" (ibid). The importance of living and working with emotions as we move through life takes on a particular importance when we reckon with their role in the fashioning and coordination of political activity. Courage, Arendt noted, is "the most elemental political attitude" (1998, p.35), and as many have stated, is not the absence of fear but living in the face of it. In politics, as in life, fear looms large; an ever-present possibility to set the pulse racing. In *Zen in the Martial Arts*, Joe Hyams describes how he taught one of his students one particular way to handle it:

> *I will have a student practice kicking at you every day that you come in, with instructions that he is never to make contact. Until your fear of being kicked becomes familiar and you develop confidence, stand still and do not react. In time you will no longer be afraid. This I promise you.* (1982, p.104)

Safety is paramount in the learning taking place here – but also the courage of the student to accept the challenge. Courage is not the willingness to die, but the willingness to live.

Milgram argued that the psychological was linked to the political through obedience, but this is not the only route and certainly not the most important. There is scope too for enlisting the more noble human possibilities, of which courage is one. How then are our hopes, dreams, fears, anxieties, expectations, frustrations and losses enlisted with our imaginative faculties under the condition of courage to make the work of policy and action? Love, compassion, sympathy, boldness, fearlessness, fun and imagination are vital to alternative ways of seeing and being in the world and consequently vital to action in it.

Many systems of martial-arts training have sought to cultivate these qualities – bringing together spiritual development, self-defence and from Buddhism the notion of "right conduct." The Shaolin moral code for example comprises twelve ethics, ten forbidden acts and ten obligations.[42] Patience, insight and calmness accordingly are likewise considered pre-requisites of good Kung Fu (Ke-Wit, 1981). The training of character and the disciplining and harnessing of emotion central to Kung Fu are directly related to its Buddhist antecedents. Accordingly these are embedded in a philosophy that emphasises conduct in harmony with the world – not the fragmented and piecemeal world of the natural sciences but the world of continuous flow and transformation – "the secret to living life" (Slingerland, 2014, p.154).

Explaining the nature of this ceaseless process of becoming is not the goal. Rather than reducing the world to some idealised conceptual abstraction, the task becomes how to manage one's time within this "'fluid continuity' of the real" (Middleton & Brown, 2005, p.82). Through one's physical training, one learns to deal with this flux and to align oneself with respect to the currents active in the world; to "fit in" with the universe, either by engaging, controlling or deflecting force or retreating before it; to let go and move on when appropriate; to not "push the river" (Kozma, 2013, p.77) when faced with overwhelming force or manifest destiny. Strategy, timing and distance – all are vital as one negotiates with the changing contours of personal and social space and the expansions and contractions of time that define moments of emotional significance (Payne, 1997). Movement (of one's body and one's awareness) becomes the dynamic metaphorical template for appraising and guiding action. In sparring, touch, awareness, memory and movement blend imperceptibly into one, corroborating Bergson's judgement that "perception has its true and final explanation in the tendency of the body to movement" (2002, p.125). The "choices" of how and when to act are thereby not made in one's head but in one's total being. "Enacted" thought is thus embodied, a boundary-less awareness which can be cultivated through martial-arts training and meditation as well as facilitated in a variety of different social environments.

Bergson is not alone in linking perception to movement. A

similar notion underpins Gibson's (2015) ecological theory of "direct perception" or "optic flow." For Gibson much of our perception can be understood in terms of a confluence between optic flow patterns and our own physical movement through space. The ambient environment provides rich and complex patterns of stimuli which afford us opportunities for action that do not require complex cognitive processes or interpretation. This is clearly evident in the rapidity of move and countermove in experienced martial artists in which there is insufficient time to process the incoming stimuli to any great depth. Where perceptual input is processed further this involves extracting what is invariant in the stimulus flux. Bergson, Gibson and the martial artist all deal with knowledge on an intuitive rather than symbolic level. Their collective insights suggest a different way for viewing our interaction with the environment – one not predicated on the metaphor of biological computer (see Epstein, 2016).

The philosophy and practice of Kung Fu is a realisation of a principle espoused by Henry Bergson – that "a theory of knowledge and a theory of life [... are] inseparable" (2007, p.xxxvii). Reality as perpetual fluid continuity and transformation lies at the heart of Bergson's (2002) philosophical works. Bergsonian thought, long neglected in psychology, is a venture into the nature of time, existence, memory and consciousness. As argued here, it calls for an entirely different mode of psychological enquiry – creative, qualitative, intuitive and practical – connected with the actuality of one's life in the present, always-passing moment. A considerable obstacle to doing so is our habitual cultivated emphasis on conscious control, cognition, logic, will power and striving – the disembodied mind with its attendant obedient body. This is the psychological framework at the heart of both Cartesian thought and capitalism.[43]

Slingerland (2003, 2014, 2015) sees in the ethical void and crisis of thought that pervade contemporary life, an opportunity to once more engage with the philosophical systems of the East which emphasise belonging, community, meaning and an acceptance of a greater whole. Not surprisingly (or perhaps surprisingly?) some psychotherapists have seen value in applying these principles in psychotherapy and counselling. Laing himself thought martial arts should occupy a pivotal place in psychotherapy training. One obvious advantage to this would be less fear of difficult or disturbed people and consequently less desire to impose drug regimes in order to subdue or control. Arguably the physical self-confidence that comes from martial-arts training could free therapists from acting on the basis of any fear they might have of physical attack. Belief in the dangerousness of those who seek mental-health services is a prominent stereotype which, if rendered inactive, would likely entail a reduction in the numbers of clients tranquilised to calm the therapist's fears. Handling one's fear – not allowing it to freeze the mind – is certainly of crucial importance but it is not restricted to dealing with physical danger.

In modern societies the fear of thinking is arguably as widespread as the fear of physical attack and the risks just as great. Unrestrained thinking has come to be associated with fear of disapproval or fear of the outcome of thinking itself – i.e. the notion that there are some things that shouldn't be thought at all. Laing took as a marker of the "psychophobic" nature of Western culture, an intolerance of the divergent possibilities of thought, mood and experience; a stance that declares "unreason" to be the enemy of the controlled and conscious execution of reason. The human capacity to think anew is a hallmark of creativity and if we are to escape from our current dire predicament it will be sorely needed. We will also need the realisation that thought is a spontaneous effortless activity; an integral part of the ebb and flow of reality – it does not require conscious effort, though it may sometimes be aided and directed by it. Doing without striving; performance as non-action, cultivated in a state of no-mindedness.[44] Chinese thought refers to this as *Wu-wei*

(Slingerland, 2014). Bergson articulated a similar principle of "le bon sens" – "a strange hidden power" (Bergson, 2002, p.430), a harmonising of intellect, will, passion, ethics and action to negotiate our relations with the world, which confer protection from "intellectual automatism" (Bergson, cited in Mullarkey, 1999, p.5). In contrast, tied to Cartesian dualism, we lack a suitable unifying term to encompass the wisdom of embodied-action. Rooted to the spot we entertain a multitude of disjointed cognitive concepts: "openness to experience," "common sense" and "intelligence." All of them neglect the physical actuality of our moving existence in the world; all these attributes are considered to be localised within the individual and it is demanded of all psychologists and educators that they be measurable through simple paper-and-pencil tests. Philosophy has in general fared little better, though Arendt's distinction between thought and cognition (and logical reasoning), does capture some of the elements of Wu-wei. "Cognition," she writes, "always has a definite aim," while "thought on the contrary, has neither an end nor an aim outside itself" (1998, pp.170-1). Schopenhauer (1995) expressed a similar notion when he argued that we can do as we will but not will as we will.

Slingerland identifies two distinct strands of ancient Chinese teaching concerning how best to attain the state of Wu-wei. One is the conscious, ritualistic, arguably rigid, striving adherence to tradition and standard social values, exemplified by Confucius; the other is the Taoist/Buddhist spontaneous and selfless surrender to the "Way" – as found in the works of Chuang Tzu and Lao Tzu. Both "schools" of thought assume a natural ordered state to the world and advance elaborate ideas on human nature; a human nature conceived not as something opposed to nurture but as action – what we do in the world.[45] A consistent theme in both philosophical traditions is how goodness can best be culti-vated – indeed there is a concern in both on what the nature of goodness is.[46] Confucianist, Taoist and Buddhist doctrines remain alive in much martial-arts practice – the varied paths toward enlightenment paved with the rigours of discipline and technique (Wile, 2007; Crudelli, 2008). The Taoist influence can perhaps most keenly be discerned where the expressed goal of many years of practice is the cultivation of the practitioners' own free form – a form without form, congruent with the belief that each of us fits with the world in a unique way. In sparring, one meets oneself as well as one's opponent. In so doing the fight is estranged, and in dealing with the spontaneous attacks of the opponent with newly created form one transcends the seeming impossibility of perceiving the new in the familiar.

The meditative practices (and physical exercises) that inform the development of Kung Fu as well as the manifest conundrums and paradoxes of Zen koans[47] and Taoist wisdom are designed to shift one's mind from the slumbers of habitual thought. These bear the hallmarks of practices of estrangement. Just as Shklovskian estrangement is essentially an artistic method of directing conscious intent away from an analysis of the psychological meaning or logical messages in a piece of prose, so too the poetry of the Zen koan. If we recall Shklovsky's comments on the two choices facing the Soviet artist – "to write for the desk drawer or to write on state demand" – with his accompanying declaration –"there is no third alternative. Yet that is precisely the one that must be chosen" (cited in Boym, 2008, pp.20-1) – it evades common-sense understanding. Compare this with the classic Zen riddle: "'You can hear the sound of two hands when they clap together,' said Mokurai. 'Now show me the sound of one hand'" (Reps, 1971, p.34). The solutions to both cannot be arrived at by logical analysis – indeed such analysis is an impediment. The resolution of the koans, one can't help but notice, frequently end with the raucous laughter of either the master or the student (or indeed the reader) as enlightenment is attained. Longchenpa, a fourteenth-century Tibbetan Buddhist, wrote:

Since everything is but an apparition,
Perfect in being what it is,
Having nothing to do with good or bad,
Acceptance or rejection,
One may well burst out in laughter (cited in Zukav, 1984, p.297)[48]

Enlightenment should not be understood as a permanent state of affairs akin to some psychological utopia but as an understanding in one's being – a fully embodied knowledge – that one is at least temporarily aligned with the complexities (and simplicities) of our social existence in the world. The knowledge is expressed in the simultaneous emotional (and cognitive) letting-go and acceptance of a larger truth – a surrender to the action systems of the world (Slingerland, 2014). Shklovsky's solution to mental strangulation by the Soviet system was the non-linear zig-zag of the knight's move, "distance and difference the secret tonic to creativity" (Lehrer, cited in Kleon, 2013, p.923). Opening his collection of essays he remarked: "In Russia everything is so contradictory that we have all become witty in spite of ourselves" (Shklovsky, 2005, p.4). He finished his collection with the following epigram: "This is the end of the knight's move. *The knight turns its head and laughs*" (ibid, p.131; italics in original). Laughter is perhaps one of our best forms of knowledge – artists and comedians have long cultivated it. It belongs at the heart of any psychology. "Real laughter, beyond joking, mockery, ridicule," allows us, as Kundera wrote, "to live profoundly" (1996, p.79).

Off-Modern Feeling

We find estrangement and its link to cognitive reorganisation and emotional release in such diverse activities and cultures as Zen Buddhism (meditation and martial arts), Russian formalism, arts, humour, counselling and psychotherapy. This is no accident. Its extensive appearance across diverse cultures, times and contexts denotes a quintessential creative aspect of human psychology, which enables us to combat the paralysis of both thought and culture; to bring fluidity to the frozen orders of personal and political life. It opens a path to an undisclosed space from which new activity may burst forth. It is no accident therefore that Boym (2010) championed it as a vital ingredient of our human freedom and a continual reminder of the fragility and endurance of that freedom; a gift for us that is as ineradicably social and political as it is within our individual capacity to exercise it upon a wider social stage.

Even if we were to take the position that the individual psyche is entirely socially mediated and fashioned – a history of the world interiorised in the mind – the actuality of our experience, what Dennet (1991) referred to as qualia, the experience of experiencing, is not shared. In the vastness of the world, each of us singularly resides in the centre of our own experience of it. As Laing (1968) noted, each of us is limited to *our* experience only. In relation to any other person we only directly experience their behaviour, which may of course be a consequence of how they experience the world including us. Beyond the singular other, our collective experiences are inter-related and refracted through behaviour, language, culture and history. The nature of that refraction is critically dependent on place; where we are in the world and how we spend our time there.

The entirety of the humanities and social sciences are an attempt to fathom and comprehend the tensions and relationships that exist between this individual private[49] world of experience and the unbroken inter-connected reality of the world in which we swim. In the chasm that separates psychology from the social sciences this is the gap that we seek to bridge. At the same time our experience, both of others directly and indirectly shaped by others, is what bridges it and makes of it an unbroken unity. As a child, looking at the index finger of my right hand, I wondered where I ended and the rest of the world began. But there is no point of separation in the interconnected matrix of being, where the whole cannot be understood without the individual human actors who collectively create it – and where we as individuals cannot be comprehended without the context of the whole. There is thus no beginning and no end. Our bodies exist always in relation to what we think of as beyond them. The movement between these poles, between us and the world, is not a bidirectional series of causal influences but a simultaneous concurrent one. The mistake and the puzzle stems from our ingrained linguistic habits which situate us in the world as objects. Despite the indisputable fact of our subjective centres of awareness, psychology has largely accentuated this objectification and forgotten that our presence in the world is as actors. As Socrates asserted, to be is to do.

Away from the stringent and stultifying confines of academic psychology are a variety of quite different disciplines. Here "discipline" can be considered to mean not just a branch of academic knowledge but a system for training and teaching – a set of transformative practices for enabling students/practitioners to grow in skill, awareness and knowledge, and to move along in tune with the world and the notes it plays. Most academic knowledge is rarely considered in this way – as training for the embodied mind; one is instead expected to dispassionately contemplate prospective knowledge and mysteriously arrive at some truth without engaging emotionally or physically or in any practical way whatsoever with what lies before or behind us. Psychotherapy occasionally manages to be different – in its practice as well as in discourse. Laing's approach extended beyond the intellectual, seeking to convey ideas not through logical sparring but by engaging and stimulating emotional reactions designed to break through whatever it was in a client's/reader's character – in the immediacy of the moment – that was hindering a more fluid way of approaching things. An accomplished pianist, he would often use music to circumvent the rational blockades on feeling to achieve this. The management, disciplining and harnessing of emotion is at the centre of a number of approaches: martial arts, Buddhist meditation, co-counselling, reading, dance, theatre. Indeed it may be fundamental to all arts and literature. One of the principal arguments of the present work is that the common thread linking this vast repertoire is estrangement; that it can be found within any viable manifesto for psychological and social survival.

Where official psychology has sought to engage with the fabric of everyday life, either in literature or the broader culture, it has usually gotten no further than the asylum or the psychotherapy consulting room – both testimonial sites to our desperation to deal with human emotions and the deep currents of life that they carry. We arrive in the world effused with emotion – our primary means of relating to whomever and whatever is around us – to begin a lifelong engagement with attempts to harness and control our feelings. At the core of our own intellectual traditions, the desire to discipline and restrain feeling has resulted in a fearful neglect of the heart and a lopsided educational curriculum. While we must be circumspect with the lure of Romanticism,[50] how we make common cause with our emotional life has been the elephant in the room for any practical psychology for quite some time. Laying the foundation stones for an off-modern narrative of human connexion invites us to revisit and rework our off-loaded and buried sentiments, inclinations and emotions, that we may reach a different rapprochement with the beasts of reason.

Before we are out of primary school our interactions with the digital world have already reached a level of frightening sophistication, yet by the time the period of mandatory state education is behind us – to say nothing of university – most know nothing about what to do when confronted by a knot in the stomach, the gentle feel of a tear in the eye, the dangerous unpredictability of now, or the impending descent of red mist. It is unfortunate indeed that the cultural positioning of contending with emotion has located it within the jurisdiction of the mental-health system and not the everyday world of human relationships. Anyone hoping to deal constructively with their emotional life on its own terms and who wishes to avoid walking straight into the arms of a conceptual (or literal) straightjacket must learn to confront, adapt to or even sidestep the mental-health industries.

At all levels of the social strata, be it a family, workplace, community or nation, the system in place is defended by a convention of misinformation, mismanaged memory and brute force (Roberts & Hewer, 2014). Each of these possesses their own strategic system of games, rules and meta-rules and the means to hide them (Laing, 1971). In light of this we should at least remain attuned to the possibility that all psychological breakdown (or breakout, breakthrough) is a comment on the politics of the relationships in which we are embedded, enmeshed, intertwined or even trapped. This notion is reminiscent of Bateson's double-bind theory of "schizophrenia," advanced in the 1950s, utilised by Laing in the 1960s and '70s, and discarded from official chronicles of scientific progress since at least the 1980s. The serial invalidation hypothesis of thought disorder formulated by personal construct theorists (Bannister & Fransella, 1971) vanished from the psychological airways around the same time. Such speculation or insight, however one approaches it, remains "off" the beaten track in a biologically obsessed mainstream with a direct line to the mass media. It marches to a different rhythm. But it was not always so. Laing originally envisaged his family studies as the leading edge of modernity, concluding the introduction to *Sanity, Madness and the Family* with his assertion that here was a paradigm shift "no less radical than the shift from a demonological to a clinical viewpoint 300 years ago" (Laing & Esterson, 1964, p.13). The renowned psychoanalyst John Bowlby thought it the most important book published on families in the twentieth century (Burston, 1996), but that didn't prevent it from vanishing into academic obscurity, an empirical demonstration of the catastrophe that ensues when meaning is collectively exiled from social action and reappropriated in the disguised and tattered clothing of biological malfunction.

The war on memory is eternally with us and inscribed upon the social fabric. Awareness of it rises episodically from the depths in times of social trauma. Different cultures at different times are conscripted into it. It is one of the obstacles to any attempt to forge a history of the people of the world. One reason racism reappears and strangles social and political space is that we have failed to fully grasp the ongoing nature of our battles with memory. People of my generation – the post-war, never-had-it-so-good generation – were instructed that "Never Again" must be the rallying cry of all future generations. In the midst of this we were *de facto* being instructed to forget what we most needed to learn: how to protect ourselves from racism, hate and scapegoating when the contours of economic and social life take us beyond the cliff edge and when social institutions, desperate to maintain a disintegrating status quo, turn darkly right. This reflection is prompted in the immediate aftermath of the UK's referendum vote on EU membership (June 2016). The circumstances call to mind, as Boym (2001) so deftly did, the dangers of restorative nostalgia. In the UK this nostalgia is for empire, the imagined simplicity of past global and white supremacy. Nostalgia, Boym said, is the price we pay for modernity. A regression from modernity, sometimes in the form of barbarism, is likewise the price that can be paid for summoning the ghosts of political nostalgia. In the West it used to be that we wished to escape from the immediacy of now to the imagined future. But now the collective drive is to return to the past of fantasy. Psychology always has some bearing on these escape plans, as it too is not rooted in the present. Kirsner asked "how could knowledge without love yield knowledge of love" (2015, p.148).

We might similarly ask how memory without love can yield memory of love or indeed how hate-fuelled forgetting can yield a hate of forgetting.

Kundera's epigram that the struggle of people against power is the struggle of memory over forgetting is a truism, long etched into the substance of artistic life. The possibility for a wider understanding – an understanding in practice – of the devastating consequences of tortured, distorted and misconceived communication is not inevitably foreclosed. Still, on the current misplaced highway of biological psychiatric quasi-fascist modernity, it is important to be mindful that even on a clear day, with a full tank of fuel and the road stretching ahead, one can sometimes be lost. Psychology as an epistemological undertaking has been lost for quite some time. In pursuit of the off-modern it may always be useful to entertain a degree of scepticism, even when in possession of a map, as any user of a satellite-navigation system will know. In such circumstances, the venture "off-road" may be more fruitful. Off the beaten track of psychological knowledge is an opportunity to discover anew what it is we really want to find out about our contingent, conditioned, miraculous existence.

Faced with the existence of state prescriptions for how we are to respond behaviourally, cognitively and emotionally to the slings and arrows of life's outrageous and painful fortunes – prescriptions that are increasingly recognised as "bullshit" even by those formerly charged with drawing them up[51] – what is the knight's move? Perhaps in an off-modern psychology it needs to be doubly reflexive, a leap through four dimensions not three, in order to arrive safely at a place where we are unafraid to entertain divergent ways and modes of thinking; where a degree of accommodation with how we feel is not a luxury but an ever-present possibility. This is not just about cultivating emotional literacy and escaping the clutches of the psy-patrol (formerly known as the thought police) though that is certainly part of it.

Neither is it an instruction manual and nor is it a guide to chaos, though it may be a step to where the wild things are. Amongst other things, it is a matter of making careful choices about who one trusts with one's secret beliefs and longings and how one exercises that trust. How we experience the world as well as how we engage with it has for some time been a deeply political issue. As Foucault indicated the body is politically contested and a site of protest. Our thoughts and feelings constitute the frontier on which this battle is waged and form the basis for a psychology that can be constructively estranged from the status quo.

Some years back a student came to me apologetic that she had not been around for a few months as she had been sectioned under the Mental Health Act. I asked her what had happened. She explained that her relatives had taken fright once she had told them that US President Barack Obama had been trying to call her. I presumed it was not the cost of the putative transatlantic calls that caused them consternation. This reminded me of an occasion many years previously when I was teaching in the medical school at King's College. The students had been presented with a case in which a middle-aged gentleman's evident "psychosis" had been inferred from the fact that he said he had been to tea with Prince Phillip. Such claims appear aberrant only to the extent that we have already signed up to a view of the world based on impenetrable class barriers. There is a choice as to whether or not we participate in the construction and maintenance of that world. After listening to my student for a while, it seemed to me that what she was trying to tell me was that she wanted to be considered an important and worthy person, an understandable desire – a phone call from Obama without doubt would have demonstrated that, and given Obama's popularity index at the time (he had just been elected for the first time) would certainly have enhanced her kudos. My further perspective on her presidential musings was that she needed to consider the effects of her pronouncements on other people – in particular whether they were able to comfortably deal with them. It was a matter of trusting who you shared what with. Trust is a big deal, I opined, and asked her to think about it. The next time I saw her she appeared much happier and told me she was no longer under the immediate threat of a section order.

The varieties of alienation and dislocation from and in the world and the social-psychiatric sanctions against waking up from them constitute an extremely effective trap for maintaining the illusion that there is no alternative to the present – and that the capitalist-realist "psy" machine has in some sense been ordained by nature. Heraclitus's statement, that the world is common to those who are awake, may appeal to common sense but beyond the perception of material objects in it there is little truth to commend it. It is important to remember that the human world is not viewed in common and that, with respect to the perception of it, there are degrees of wakefulness. There is no psychiatric or psychological term for failing to realise one's actions are performed in the service of others. To be a slave and not to realise it, is still to be a slave. To be so alienated that one does not realise it, is the *sine qua non* of prescribed "normality." Marx was unable to envisage any satisfactory escape from the clutches of alienation save through wholesale transformation of the society. However, to realise that one is alienated, dislocated or marginalised from the not-so-happy-go-lucky violence of everyday life offers the real possibility of estrangement *for* the world.

One of the purposes of this book has been to present a way of approaching the human condition that is premised on a careful disengagement from the ways we currently make and perform psychological knowledge. It is to estrange psychology and renew the desire to know ourselves that we inherited from Greek culture. As old certainties fall by the wayside and a new society and new ways to live struggle to emerge, the time is ripe for a new psychological adventure. This will require neither isolated individual contemplation nor a dedication to science. We can discover and learn through unselfconsciously doing, playing, inventing and remaining engaged with others, all along attuning ourselves to the rhythms of the world that exist beyond the powers of our will.

> *Humans are the most intelligent of beings, yet they change their attitudes in various unequal ways, because the real director is not present. If people would get the sense of the real director, then they would not be guided by the subjective psyche, but would spontaneously be on the Way.* (Reps, 1971, p.162)

Off the beaten and well-worn tracks of knowledge lie opportunities to reorient ourselves to the spaces, times and places in which we live, to contribute to the fate of the world and to discover once more the artistry of the human soul.

Seven

After Words and Last Words

Books are solitudes in which we meet
– Rebecca Solnit (2013, p.54)

Art without compassion don't avail
– Stevie Smith (1978, p.163)

Svetlana Boym (2001) bequeathed us a history of nostalgia and Theodore Zeldin (1998) an "intimate" history of human relationships and emotions.[52] Both works reflect a global immersion into culturally shaped landscapes of feeling, following the political and economic earthquakes of recent years – the collapse of communism in the late twentieth century and the banking crisis and neoliberal catastrophes of the twenty-first. The shock waves from both show no sign of quiescence. The global dis-inhibition of feeling is one factor behind the rise of "psychopathic" political violence perpetrated by disillusioned alienated youth who follow the call of Jihad. Feelings are at work here in other ways. When Andy Warhol famously declared that in the future everybody will be famous for fifteen minutes, he could not have anticipated what would follow our descent into psychic numbness after years of exposure to the phenomenon. Nowadays, thoroughly bored and saturated with the trivial and transitory fame promulgated in reality TV shows for feats of breath-taking ordinariness, the profoundly alienated turn to extremist violence in order to kick off the shackles of anaesthesia and have their moment in the sun – even if they are no longer alive to bask in it (see Staufenberg, 2016).

Boym's and Zeldon's work can be considered as pioneer projects to reinvent, or indeed invent, a historically bounded psychological sensibility. In this new guise it becomes the study and lived practice (praxis) of humanity's relationship with itself (taking in the mediating terrains of the imaginary, the symbolic, the avowedly emotional and the downright real); this in the context of its geographical and historical resting places and the various ways in which we come to know our own – the human – condition. "Know thyself" (Σαυτονισθι) was one of the maxims said to have been given by Apollo's Oracle of Delphi. It was considered a warning to those entering the sacred temple to be mindful of their place. All psychologies, properly considered, are ways of knowing ourselves or at least attempts to do so; they imply not merely values but codes of conduct in the world. To know oneself in the world therefore is to uphold an ethic not only of contemplation but of critical reflective action; to know that one does not in fact fully know, that the world and we ourselves are open to discovery. Positioning the variety of modes and types of human relationship as central to understanding humanity invites a dissolution of many academic boundaries found in the house of the social sciences – no bad thing in itself – but it also cautions us against accepting the dreams of generations of scientists that knowledge can be unified into a single code or even a single language.

Bannister and Fransella, in more optimistic times, promoted a vision of psychological experimentation as "acts of imagination" (1970, p.193) – an endeavour more akin to the experiments "which novelists undertake," possibly unpublishable and which might leave no public record, but which involve the opportunity for meaningful reflection or engagement with the world. In a similar spirit, Jones challenged the preconception that the only valid form of knowledge should be "abstract disembodied, purely rational and objective" (2005, p.207). He called for a greater place for emotion and action in articulating how and what we know of "being in the world." Such epistemological experiments in living would produce learning and change, not results, and likely wash away forever what Polyanni referred to as the "desert of trivialities" engendered by passionless enquiry (1962, p.135). They raise serious questions about the purpose and direction of traditional academic analysis. This "art of knowledge" is an unfulfilled dream. It is the subject matter of the present off-modern inquiry. Under this umbrella we would become the authors and subjective centres of our own knowledge, not the objects of it; thus there would no longer be one psychology but as many variants of it as there are people. The one become many.

How might this work as a project that is simultaneously personal, social, historical, educational and political? A psychological project for anyone might then be envisaged as a personal project oriented to making sense of their life (as well as those about them), exploring amongst other things the philosophical, literary, cultural, historical, familial, dramatic, political, economic and biographical frameworks that surround and infuse it. Thus it becomes an ongoing personal authentic exploration of self, an attempt to know oneself, to discover the mythology of one's life (and that of others with it), to piece together how one has become who one is at that moment prior to further becoming.

This is a marriage of method with adventure. As both it would have the beauty and merit of being unique to each "explorer," thereby creating a space for a set of alternative narratives and performances for negotiating the slipstreams of life. This adventure gives due respect to the "miracle" of human "individuality," but takes one "off-road" from the discipline of psychology by not privileging the psychological above other modes or frameworks of "explanation," interpretation and action. It also does not privilege what are deemed to be the accepted "problems" within an academic tradition at any one time. This allows for working in ways that transcend disciplinary boundaries and favoured modes of representation within them, ways that permit one to be simultaneously reflective, passionate, poetic, individual and social. It might be as much a journey inwards as outwards or even sideways for that matter. The Beatles once sang "Your inside is out and your outside is in," a reflection on the destabilising and estranging of one's favoured axes of orientation for meeting reality; a lyrical acknowledgement that the boundaries separating different modes and realms of existence are not what they seem – at least not what we might expect from the socially constructed versions of normality we are implored not to question. Social constructionism in fact suggests such realignment as a theoretical possibility but as a purely cognitive outlook it provides no practical guides, rules of thumb or meeting places in social or political space for accomplishing this. Social constructionism often appears to be an idea that cannot be understood until one moves beyond trying to grasp it intellectually.

The adventurous method could extend to exploring influences not yet felt or active – i.e. the obscured potentialities of the past and the unripe possibilities of the future. Sometimes one may come to understand oneself better by appreciating the paths not taken – the roads not merely less travelled but not travelled at all, whether by accident, intention or force of circumstance. These counterfactual realities can be considered as perennial possible influences on the present. Life is often determined not by what is done but by what is not done. Human memory and imagination seem built to explore these side alleys and unrealised "what ifs," particularly in search of relief from accumulated pains and losses. The emphasis on realism in the science of the soul has stood in the way of this return to the unrealised past in order to move on to what might be. If one is prepared to sacrifice or suspend the notion of scientific realism, the cherished ideas of whoever or whatever one thinks one is, then the doors are opened to discover other possibilities of being.[53] A good deal of fluidity and flexibility is a vital ingredient in not only tempering the effects of the dark times in one's life but also of revealing the sources of light.

Psychology in short could be made a work of art, celebrating what Eduardo Galeano (1992, p.121) refers to as the "marriage of heart and mind," approaching discovery, knowing and learning with "sentipensante" (feeling-thinking). These suggestions carry echoes of a strand of thought that can be traced back to Epictetus, the Greek slave. For him the proper subject matter of philosophy was each person's life with the desired outcome of such study being refinements in "the art of living" (Arendt, 1978, p.154) – in one's own action in the world and self-understanding. Contrary to Epictetus, however, there is nothing here to prevent the exercise of co-operation and co-creation – as people's "individual" projects interface with others' – moving in and out of collective phases of enquiry and action in a personal-social (even political) dialectical merry-go-round. Galeano speaks of turning loose the voices so that dreams can be unshackled and undreamt, a means to turn loose other kinds of reality into the world.

Human progress has always depended on such counterfactual passions. There is nothing inherent in the above suggestion that would preclude journeying into contemporary and traditional areas of psychological enquiry – albeit the journey would need to be undertaken with a very different kind of map. In discussing this idea with a colleague, I was asked the question: "What if somebody saw themselves as a biologically programmed organism?" There is nothing inherently problematic in this (at least not from the point of view of method) – people must after all remain free to choose how they see themselves, as well as having their own starting points of enquiry. In utilising an open and systematic (a cultural-phenomenological) form of enquiry, the ontological status of the assumption would necessarily be bracketed, ripe for scrutiny with a genealogical eye to reveal its history and context. For example, in the case above: the history of technological influences on human self-image; an examination of its merits and problems; its socio-political and cultural ramifications; the implications for interpersonal life; and the paradoxes of free will that ensue not just from adopting the position but from enquiring into it. A healthy realisation that the world is not the linguistic template we have superimposed on it may be one port of call on the way; psychology relinquishing its role as a standardised commercial enterprise may ultimately be another. An inevitability in these quests to know thyself is that the "data" one gathers and "processes" may frequently escape verbalisation, and the method used to gather the data may be a form of action beyond words.

After Words

There are occasions when it seems easier than usual for us to suspend disbelief in the world in front of us; when we daydream for example or engage in its lengthier equivalent during the hours of night. Sometimes our moments of suspended thought are responses to the seemingly incredible passing before our eyes – occasioned by both the joys and pains bestowed by fate. These are mirror-image moments when our critical faculties take a holiday from the hustle and bustle of managing the impossibility of our daily lives. On one side of this mirror we fail to disbelieve the phenomenal world and on the other side we fail to believe in the evidence of our senses and what they show of our attendant share of good or bad luck. In our night life we substitute one form of improbability for another, no questions asked. In our daily endeavours we may struggle with the highly probable and certain. Between these two extremes there are occasions, and not infrequent at that, when the suspension of belief or disbelief is not deserted by the critical weight of thought, when uncertainty reigns and must be endured. Often these are moments of fear, but a specific class of such moments of uncertainty reside in times lost in reading and writing – navigating the written world of words in the former case and in the latter charting a course through it. We speak of moments lost in thought – but these are rather gains, in imagination, knowledge and storytelling capacity.

My own history of storytelling began as a recipient, naturally enough, when I was young. My father, of Amerindian heritage, would regale me with accounts of various adventures in the jungles of South America. I can't now remember how many were real and how many dreamed up, but many of them were certainly acts of imagination. Various animal characters made friends and enemies beneath the canopy, encountered problems and resolved them over the course of one or more nights. My favourite character, who regularly appeared, was called Freddie Frog. He lay in suspended animation for many years until I resurrected him one evening with Svetlana, telling her a story as we walked across Embankment Bridge in London. I have always enjoyed storytelling – putting life's and one's own exploits, twists and turns into an ongoing melee of the definite, the strange and the unexpected. Each one enters a unique branch of the unknown, often finding there desired and unanticipated riches and dreadful and unimagined injustices. Though as human beings we are creatures of great impulse when it comes to storytelling, the art is not cultivated in contemporary psychology. Nor is it generally appreciated for its significance, not only for saying something about our nature but also for building and developing relationships of mutual learning. In the stories of our lives we are, as Isabel Allende noted, both "spectators and protagonists" (1991, p.3), embedded within the stories of others and extras in the still bigger stories of time, places and époques, caught up in the grand movements of the world.

Strange as this may sound, psychology is currently also almost unique amongst the humanities and social sciences for discouraging both reading and writing books. The journal article has been put on a pedestal as the gold standard for imparting knowledge. Somewhat unfortunately this elevation has the consequence, whether intended or not, of negating the worth of extended arguments and with it creating an intellectual culture that is restricted in breadth and context. Entering what Rebecca Solnit describes as "the strange life of books" (2013, p.54) is a journey into terra incognita, an opportunity to map and find one's way in another world. This is so whether one makes the journey as a reader or a writer. Austin Kleon (2012) implored his readers to write the book they want to read – sound advice! But would anyone want to write something they would not want to read?! Sadly much of our formal education is doing precisely that, inhibiting and submerging the creative impulse rather than nurturing and promoting it. All writing is storytelling – even the boring or seemingly boring texts that fill the pages of scientific journals. They all have beginnings, middles and endings, though they are seldom constructed in their presented order and seldom appear in their true order. Storytelling however is not only about writing, nor even movement. We know that images and pictures tell a thousand tales.

Considered as a story, science has always been about more than the accumulation of facts. It is instead a fable of the elusive search for understanding. Facts of course are supposed to be items of knowledge and truth, whose presence in the world is beyond dispute. Facts however are always disputed – and today's collection only attained their status through possessing a successful lineage of storytelling, one that not only accounted successfully for observed data and saw off opposition but made headway beyond the shores of the imagination. This is another way of affirming the central place that the art of rhetoric or persuasion has in the production of knowledge. There are other possibilities. We can become comfortable with not knowing what comes next. No ultimate truths to find. "Walking into darkness," Rebecca Solnit called it (2013, p.185), suspending ourselves between one moment and the next and then the next. For the Chinese this is an aspect of Wu-wei; for the artist, fluid, estranged movement.

Walking into darkness is not sleep-walking, it is the spontaneous carriage of the past into the present and from there the future. This spontaneity can be curtailed in the face of emotionally challenging information. Fear is one such source. The more we fear "fear," the more its icy grip enfolds us. What is the mass psychology of fear and how do we discern the useful from the not-so-useful examples of our responses to it? Kelly framed fear cognitively as "the awareness of an imminent incidental change in one's core structures" (Bannister & Fransella, 1970, p.206), but it is so much more than this. Largely undiscussed professionally, we are habitual witnesses to people's attempts to deal with it – from cinemagoers hooked on the pleasures of laughing and screaming during the regular fright night, to the shocked victims of traffic accidents and other forms of trauma, where we see people sweating heavily and shaking uncontrollably. In the pantheon of acceptable public behaviour, laughter is just about in; screaming outside the cinema certainly is not. Uncontrollable shaking is on the proscribed list wherever it occurs. To promote fearlessness requires that we cultivate it, teach it and in some sense systematically estrange it as "policy" in our coordinated and public responses to all those features of the world that incite fright and terror – whether accidentally or through the systematic operations, practices and legacies of power that promote it and instil oppression and passivity.

In the wake of the London bombings of 2005 two websites were set up: www.iamfuckingterrified.com and www.wereshit-tingourselves.com (see Harper, Roberts & Sloboda, 2007). These are important acknowledgements that fear can be publically admitted, "de-privatised" and estranged. For fearlessness to flourish we must accept feeling afraid, learn to work with it, against it, aside it and through it, opening up for deliberation a panoply of feeling, planning, action and inaction. In short, how we meet with it and greet it – a detour into the unexplored poten-tialities of terror and our responses to it. This brings us to another paradox: only by accepting the presence of fear can we become free of its effects. The significance of this is that we might even come to welcome it. Courage in the face of fear is the logic of a call to arms to resist illegitimate authority – to resist the stifling demands of physical, intellectual and psychological conformity, all of which are rooted in the legal, educational and mental-health systems. How we learn to do so ought to occupy a much higher priority in political movements than is presently the case, and also of course a more prominent place in psychological instruction.

Some of our confusion around these issues can be illustrated by a thought experiment I ran with medical students on a psychiatry firm. Most of the future doctors readily agreed that a hypothetical patient who entered the surgery laughing must have encountered something at least mildly amusing in the waiting room. As soon as I lengthened the period of imaginary laughter beyond a few seconds, however, the students sought immediately to medicalise it with an ensuing therapeutic sanction proposed, aimed at stopping it. When they were asked to contemplate someone screaming or shaking making their way through the door, the imagined patient faced immediate sanction. The medical students' confusion, and much of ours, lies in the mistake of equating the stopping of a behaviour or emotion with the end of the harm it is associated with. As we have discussed, the arts of estrangement have been overlooked in psychotherapy, although they have an important part to play in the task of freeing us from the individual and collective ills of twenty-first-century life. They belong as part of a radical program to breathe new life into education, psychology, psychotherapy and political protest – the major avenues of personal and collective transformation at our disposal. Such a program must, as a priority, aim to detoxify and eliminate the semi-automatic urge to turn to racism in times of economic crisis. It is the lesson not learnt from the 1930s; the reason "Never Again" has given way so often to "Here we go again."

In a decaying society, art, if it is truthful, must also reflect these signs of decay and in keeping with its social function show the world as changeable – thus helping to change it. Psychology can be part of that effort. This book has not asked why change is possible, because it has taken change to be the fundamental currency of reality. Off the beaten track, artistic endeavour, invention, play and adventure promise a form of psychological practice that is capable of moving with this fluid continuity of the real. This would be a practice where epistemology and ontology fuse into one; a singular undertaking into the unknown.

Science can find no individual enjoyment in nature: Science can find no aim in nature: Science can find no creativity in nature; it finds mere rules of succession [...] science only deals with half the evidence provided by human experience [...] The disastrous separation of body and mind which has been fixed on European thought by Descartes is responsible for this blindness of science. (Whitehead, 1968, p.154)

Psychology, like the society in which it is embedded, is in crisis. It faces perhaps its greatest challenge. Its boundaries and aspirations must be redrawn. This book is a modest effort to suggest one way in which it might be done. But let us be clear, the stakes are high. Bronowski, mindful of the horrors of the Second World War and keenly aware of the threats that knowledge can pose when out of control, in the wrong hands, and serving the wrong ends, spoke of the necessity for our intellectual commitment to work in unison with our emotional commitment. At the conclusion of his great work *The Ascent of Man*, he issued a warning that today we would do well to heed:

We must not perish by the distance between people and government, between people and power, by which Babylon and Egypt and Rome failed. And that distance can only be conflated, can only be closed, if knowledge sits in the homes and heads of people with no ambition to control others, and not up in isolated seats of power. (1973, p. 435)

Psychology must be returned to the world and refocused on the challenges of living. As the old world dies painfully around us, we feel in need of hope. Hope is different to expectation or probability – it is not to disown, forget or dismiss the possibility of the "miraculous" appearance of good amidst the chaos and cruelties of the world. It is one aspect of our leap into the uncertainties of the future; "an embrace of the unknown and the unknowable" (Solnit, 2016, p.xii). It exists to be extracted from the world as much as impending doom can be projected into it. Both are part of the real – and must be kept in appropriate balance. The difficult trick is not to become attached to either one too much. In her articulation of the case for hope, Solnit has reminded us that a "new imagination of politics and change is already here" (ibid, p. 59). It is time for psychology to join it.

Each age is a dream that is dying, or one that is coming to birth
– Arthur O'Shaughnessy (cited in Guilfoyle, 1979, p.120)

Last Words

This is true right now.

Endnotes

1. See her text for Adam Bartos' (2001) photographic survey of the Soviet Space program.

2. The artificially intelligent life forms of this vision are usually adult, suggesting a disdain for childhood and a failure to appreciate that being human necessitates a process of becoming. It is of interest that science fiction has explored artificial intelligence and childhood – Spielberg's *AI*, based on the Brian Aldiss short story "Super-Toys Last All Summer Long," is one notable example, and Brent Spiner's interpretation of the android Data in *Star Trek*, as essentially a child-like being, is another. These representations act as reminders that human beings enter the world as innocents. This is not a favoured idea in academia, in which the ruling trope is that we are Darwinian programmed killing machines.

3. http://www.theguardian.com/education/2015/jul/06/let-uk-universities-do-what-they-do-best-teaching-and-research?CMP=share_btn_link. Accessed July 2015.

4. Remarks by MP David Davis. See: https://www.politicshome.com/party-politics/articles/story/tory-mp-parts-trade-union-bill-akin-francos-spain.

5. They argue for example that scientific psychology comes to occupy a space that was *"reserved for it* in the ideological realm" (p.53).

6. A problem which, it must be said, is not obvious to the legions of psychologists whose work fills the pages of professional journals – journals that continue their indecent obsession with hollow theory while displaying an active disdain for publishing work about the events and perspectives that do exist on the ground.

7. http://www.independent.co.uk/news/world/americas/american-psychologists-were-complicit-in-torture-after-911-

study-finds-10382136.html. Accessed July 2015.

8. Wilhelm Reich could perhaps contest this position, though Fromm's body of work can more properly be said to kick-start a discipline of political psychology.

9. And perhaps not even metaphorically speaking. Arendt however discusses how a number of philosophers and theorists – Adam Smith, Kant, Hegel, Goethe and Marx, amongst others – have postulated an unseen dynamical force acting behind "the backs of real men" to explain the development of human progress (1978, Book 2, p.153-5). But perhaps there is no progress – only the flux of imponderable and incessant change.

10. To save readers the task of reaching for a dictionary or giving up on Foucault, "intrication" means entanglement.

11. See Barthes' essay "The Death of the Author" (1977). Here Barthes argues that a text must be separated from its author to avoid interpretative tyranny. "Writing is that neutral, composite, oblique space where our subject slips away, the negative where all identity is lost, starting with the very identity of the body writing" (p.141).

12. Baudelaire is credited with coining the term "modernity." He referred to it as "the transitory, the fugitive, the contingent, the half of art of which the other half is eternal and the immutable" (cited in Boym, 2001, p.19). It is his attempt to capture the new fleeting rhythms of time and life in the burgeoning urban metropolis.

13. In the context of politics and history, Arendt was of the view that "application of the law of large numbers" signified the "wilful obliteration of their very subject matter" (1998, p.42). The same can certainly also be said of psychology.

14. Feyerabend rejected notions of a universal (across time and place) scientific method. This is consistent with different local methodological traditions in different disciplines but such a weakened variant of scientific method poses no

insuperable obstacles to merging arts and science.

15. Bennet et al. (2009) provide a humorous illustration of some of the dangers that lurk in MRI research. It is easily forgotten that the method is detecting magnetic disruption in the brain and depends upon complex data-processing algorithms which may lead to misinterpretation of background noise. Their study showed how it was possible to "detect" activity in the brain of a dead fish – the Atlantic salmon to be precise.

16. Excerpt from "Lullaby" originally published in 1937.

17. This includes the manner in which they can be known.

18. See Boym (1995, particularly pp.158-9) for a consideration of the aesthetic commemoration of the everyday art of survival in our lived personal and communal spaces. Boym's focus is on the inhabitants of Soviet living space – but the senti-mental (i.e. human) value and functional worth of her analysis extends far beyond the realm of the Soviet era and far beyond its geographical borders.

19. Perhaps three if we also include a rejection of Aristotelian logic as an absolute guide to living in the twenty-first century. If we take seriously AI theorist Marvin Minsky's aphorism that "logic does not apply to the real world" we are more than halfway there.

20. It is artistic "creativity" rather than scientific "ingenuity" that receives the lion's share of this interest. The language itself is revealing. A particularly crass example of how the obsession with creativity and madness is played out can be found in the foreword to Virginia Woolf's (2013) *To the Lighthouse*. Woolf is described by Cheshire (2013) as an artist "whose creative expression was bad for [her] health" (p.v-vi). The damaging effect of her childhood sexual abuse at the hands of her half-brother somehow gets overlooked in order to further the accusations against the creative spirit.

21. Psychology's illustrious alumni are usually male – a topic worthy of consideration in its own right.

22. Brian Patten, Adrian Henri and Roger McGough.

23. I am referring to "Yellow Submarine" of course.

24. It remains a perennial mystery to me how graffiti artists the world over all seem to possess the same handwriting.

25. Boym (2001) distinguishes between restorative nostalgia (desiring the recreation of a political past which may or may not have once existed) and reflective nostalgia (more personal, melancholic and accepting of time's irreversible flow).

26. See Coverley (2010) for a quixotic and Anglo-French-centric tour of psychogeography.

27. I have purposely omitted the famed *flâneur* from this list of urban wanderers, who – despite the seemingly eternal fame conferred by Benjamin – has never been satisfactorily defined (see Solnit, 2014, p.199). The *flâneur* can be considered a mythical figure personifying the spirit and relationship quality emblematic of capitalist modernity – a ghost among the urban masses. Hayes (2003) draws parallels between the *flâneur*'s penchant for "observation at a distance" and the alienated watchfulness that lies at the heart of much psychological research. Rather than the characteristic arrogant aloofness, which positions the psychologist as "detective of urban social life" (ibid, p.62), he argues that it is through engagement *with* those living on society's margins that psychology would be permitted to challenge its own bourgeois credentials and make of itself an ally for fruitful social change.

28. He also wrote "The First Time Ever I Saw Your Face," the song made famous by Roberta Flack.

29. Jung undertook most of the work for the *Red Book* between 1915 and 1930.

30. Nowadays it seems it is an issue for neuroscience. Lampinen (2002) for example discusses the *déjà vu* experience in the light of different memory systems being involved in

conscious recollection and feelings of familiarity. Activation of the latter without the former it is suggested may produce the experience. Currently there is no consensus in the scientific community on what the correct explanation is.

31. Re-evaluation co-counselling is a form of non-professional peer counselling that initially arose in Seattle in the 1960s. Unlike just about every other development in the counselling and psychotherapy field, co-counselling has largely existed outside the confines of academic and professional life, spreading by word of mouth and direct personal contact. It incorporates insights from both behavioural psychology and psychoanalysis whilst taking an original approach to the nature of distress and recovery from it (see text above. For a more detailed treatment see Caroline & New, 2005; Jackins, 1997).

32. It is of more than passing interest that whilst the scientific community continues to display a sceptical attitude toward catharsis, the general public retain a fascination with it (Safran & Greenberg, 1991).

33. The situation in the arts is somewhat different – a point to which I shall return.

34. See also Sue et al. where the cathartic method is referred to as a "therapeutic use of verbal expression to release pent-up emotional conflicts" (2016, p.22). Banyard et al. describe it either as the release of "built-up emotional energy" or an "unpleasant build-up of psychic energy" (2015, p.249). What these mysterious quantities of emotional and psychic energy refer to is left to the reader to decide. In social psychology the term is further debased by seemingly not even requiring the expression of any emotion at all – see Russell (1993, pp.211-36) for several illustrative examples. The theory of catharsis is rejected ion the basis that attending or participating in aggressive sports does not reduce aggression, demonstrating amongst many things an inability to distinguish stimulus

from response.

35. Boym indicates that Aristotle's remarks do not provide any clarity about the actual meaning of pity and fear for the audience (2010, p.54). On that we must speculate – but perhaps what is of greater import is acknowledging the public and significant nature of the depiction of emotion.

36. Breuer describes the procedure followed as one that "left nothing" in terms of "logical consistency and systematic implementation" (Freud & Breuer, 2004, p.39).

37. Vygotsky's premise has received some support from experimental psychology (see Adrián, Páez & Alvarez, 1996).

38. The term Reich used to describe it. It is not difficult to see why it did not catch on.

39. The concept of emotion is central to Vygotsky's work, though translation issues surround the language he used to describe emotion, feeling, mood and temperament (see Mesquita, 2012).

40. But it's not a simple as that… "To say there is a self is not true. To say there is no self is not true. Then what is true?" (Ajahn Chah, cited in Kornfield, 2008, p.77).

41. See: http://rationalwiki.org/wiki/McDojo.

42. These include the obligations to make peace, eliminate bullies and help the weak, eliminate the cruel and the villainous, protect the lonely and the oppressed, be chivalrous and generous, and right wrongs courageously (Ke-Wit, 1981).

43. See Davies (2011) for an assessment of the radical capabilities of Bergsonian, Deleuzian and Buddhist thought for challenging the neoliberal order.

44. Lee describes no-mindedness as follows. It is "not a blank mind that shuts out all thoughts and emotions; nor is it simply calmness and quietness of mind […] it is the 'non-graspingness' of thoughts that mainly constitutes the principle of no mind. A gung-fu man employs his mind as a

mirror – it grasps nothing and refuses nothing; it receives but does not keep [...] When his private ego and conscious efforts yield to a power not his own he then achieves the supreme action, non-action (wu-wei)" (1997, pp.123-4).

45. George Kelly, the creator of Personal Construct Theory, similarly envisioned us as forms of movement.

46. See Allan (2000) for an introduction to Confucian thought. There are interesting parallels to be drawn between Hegel's philosophy of spirit and the Confucian belief that the will of heaven influences the earthly progression from degenerate to more humane rulers. The idea that human nature is perfectible over time also has echoes in Marx's notion of species being and its socio-economic-historical development.

47. The Zen koan is a succinct paradoxical statement, a subject for meditation used to train monks to relinquish their dependence on reason and to push them toward enlightenment.

48. My own favourite story is the following:

"Our schoolmaster used to take a nap every afternoon," related a disciple of Soyen Shaku. "We children asked him why he did it and he told us: 'I go to dreamland to meet the old sages just as Confucious did.' When Confucious slept, he would dream of ancient sages and later tell his followers about them.

"It was extremely hot one day so some of us took a nap. Our schoolmaster scolded us. 'We went to dreamland to meet the ancient sages the same as Confucious did,' we explained. 'What was the message from those sages?' our schoolmaster demanded. One of us replied: 'We went to dreamland and met the sages and asked them if our schoolmaster came here every afternoon, but they said they had never seen any such fellow.'" (Reps, 1971, p.46)

49. Private in the sense of inaccessible to others.

50. Gjesdal (2014) challenges the accepted view of Romanticism – that a sharp unbridgeable division exists between its emphasis on individuality and a commitment to a shared education through culture.

51. See interview with Allen Francis, lead editor of *DSM IV*, in Greenberg (2011).

52. Boym's work can be seen as a revelation of the contemporary zeitgeist. Zeldon sees his account as an investigation of familiar ghosts. In need of a new vision of the past, we remain haunted by the familiar spectres of loneliness, love, desire, compassion, fear, hope and curiosity, whose trajectories he follows.

53. Lao Tzu remarked: "When I let go of what I am, I become what I might be."

References

Adrián, J.A., Páez, D. & Alvarez, A. (1996) Art, Emotion and Cognition: Vygotskian and current approaches to musical induction and changes in mood, and cognitive complexization. *Psicothema*, 8(1), pp.107-18.

Alighieri, D. (2000) *La Divina Comedia: Canti scelti.* New York. Dover Publications.

Allan, S. (2000) Introduction. In: Confucious. *The Analects.* London. Everyman Publishers.

Allende, I. (1991) *The Stories of Eva Luna.* London. Penguin.

Anderson, L. (2015) *The Heart of a Dog.* DVD. London. Dogwoof.

Arendt, H. (1976) *The Origins of Totalitarianism.* London. Harcourt.

—. (1978) *The Life of the Mind.* London. Harcourt, Inc.

—. (1998) *The Human Condition.* Chicago & London. The University of Chicago Press.

Aristotle (1996) *Poetics.* London. Penguin.

Auden, W.H. (1991) *Collected Poems.* New York. Random House.

Bannister, D. & Fransella, F. (1971) *Inquiring Man.* Harmondsworth. Penguin.

Banyard, P., Dillon, G., Norman, C. & Winder, B. (eds.) (2015) *Essential Psychology* (2nd ed.). London. Sage.

Barnard, P. & Shapiro, S. (2014) Editors' introduction to the English edition of F. Guéry & D. Deleule. *The Productive Body.* Winchester. Zero Books.

Barthes, R. (1977) *Image Music Text.* London. Harper Collins.

Baudelaire, C. (2010) *The Painter of Modern Life.* London. Penguin.

Baudrillard, J. (2008) *The Perfect Crime.* London. Verso.

Beaumont, M. (2015) *Night Walking: A nocturnal history of London.* London. Verso.

Benjamin, W. (1999) *Illuminations.* London. Pimilico.

—. (2007) *Reflections.* New York. Schocken Books.

Bennett, C.M., Baird, A.A., Miller, M.B. & George, L.W. (2009) Neural correlates of interspecies perspective taking in the post-mortem Atlantic Salmon: an argument for proper multiple comparisons correction. *Journal of Serendipitous and Unexpected Results*, 1, pp.1-5.

Berger, P. & Luckmann, T. (1967) *The Social Construction of Reality*. Harmondsworth. London.

Bergson, H. (2002) *Key Writings*. London. Bloomsbury.

—. (2007) *Creative Evolution*. Houndmills. Palgrave.

Bentall, R.P. (2004) *Madness Explained: Psychosis and human nature*. London. Allen Lane.

Billig, M. (2008) *The Hidden Roots of Critical Psychology*. London. Sage.

Blackburn, S. (2005) *Truth: A guide for the perplexed*. London. Allen Lane.

Bolleli, D. (2008) *On the Warrior's Path: Philosophy, fighting, and martial arts mythology*. Berkeley. Blue Snake Books.

Bondi, L., Davidson, J. & Smith, M. (eds.) *Emotional Geographies*. Farnham. Ashgate.

Bowman, P. (2007) Deconstruction as a Martial Art. Presented at "Counter-Movements: Institutions of Difference." Portsmouth University, UK. 24-25 July 2006.

Boym, S. (1994) *Common Places: Mythologies of everyday life in Russia*. Cambridge. Harvard University Press.

—. (2001) *The Future of Nostalgia*. New York. Basic Books.

—. (2003) Kosmos: Remembrances of the future. In: A. Bartos. *Kosmos: A portrait of the Russian space age*. New York. Princeton Architectural Press.

—. (2005) Poetics and Politics of Estrangement: Victor Shklovsky and Hannah Arendt. *Poetics Today*, 26(4), pp.581-612.

—. (2008) *Architecture of the Off-Modern*. New York. Princeton Architectural Press.

—. (2010) *Another Freedom: The alternative history of an idea*.

London. University of Chicago Press.

—. (2010b) Ruins of the Avant-Garde: From Tatlin's tower to paper architecture. In: J. Hell & A. Schönle (eds.) *Ruins of Modernity*. Durham and London. Duke University Press. pp.58-85.

—. (2010c) Off-Modern Manifestoes. *Nostalgic Technology*. http://www.svetlanaboym.com/offmodern.html.

—. (2012) Nostalgic Technologies: Multitasking with clouds. *Photoworks*, Spring/Summer, p.6-13.

Bronowski, J. (1973) *The Ascent of Man*. London. BBC.

Burak, J. (2016) Overvaluing confidence, we've forgotten the power of humility. *Aeon*. https://aeon.co/ideas/overvaluing-confidence-we-ve-forgotten-the-power-of-humility. Accessed July 2016.

Butt, T. (2008) *George Kelly: The psychology of personal constructs*. Houndmills. Palgrave Macmillan.

Calvino, I. (2007) *Invisible Cities*. London. Vintage.

Capra, F. (1975) *The Tao of Physics*. London. Flamingo.

—. (1982) *The Turning Point*. London. Flamingo.

—. (2015) *The Voice of Experience* and the emerging science. In M. Guy Thompson (ed.) *The Legacy of R.D. Laing*. London. Routledge.

Cernan, E. & Davis, D. (1999) *The Last Man on the Moon*. New York. St Martin's Griffin.

Cheshire, G. (2013) Life and Times. Introduction to V. Woolf. *To the Lighthouse*. London. Harper Press.

Chomsky, N. & Foucault, M. (2006) *The Chomsky-Foucault Debate on Human Nature*. New York and London. The New Press.

Chong, S.S.H. (2012) *The Oriental Obscene*. Duke University Press. Durham and London.

Chuang-Tzu (1993) *The Essential Tao*. Translated by Thomas Cleary. New York. Harper Collins.

Conradson, D. (2005) Freedom, Space and Perspective: Moving encounters with other ecologies. In: L. Bondi, J. Davidson &

M. Smith (eds.) *Emotional Geographies*. Farnham. Ashgate.

Coverley, M. (2010) *Psychogeography*. Harpenden. Pocket Essentials.

Crews, F. (1996) Missing the Point about Freud. In: N. R. Keddie (ed.) *Debating Gender, Debating Sexuality*. New York and London. New York University Press. pp.277-95.

Cromby, J., Harper, D. & Reavey, P. (2013) *Psychology, Mental Health and Distress*. Houndmills. Palgrave MacMillan.

Crudelli, C. (2008) *The Way of the Warrior*. London. DK.

Davies, B. (2011) Intersections between Zen Buddhism and Deleuzian Philosophy. *Psyke & Logos*, 32, pp.28-45.

Dennett, D. (1992) *Consciousness Explained*. London. Allen Lane.

Eagelton, T. (2015) The Slow Death of the University. *The Chronicle of Higher Education*. 6 April. http://www.annette-greenagency.co.uk/page_3255917.html. Accessed June 2015.

Edmond, J. (2006) Lyn Hejinian and Russian Estrangement. *Poetics Today*, 27(1), pp.97-124.

Emerson, C. (2005) Shklovesky's *Ostranenie*, Bakhtin's *Vernakhodimost*: How distance serves an aesthetics of arousal differently from an aesthetics based on pain. *Poetics Today*, 26(4), pp.637-64.

Epstein, R. (2016) The Empty Brain. *Aeon*. https://aeon.co/essays/your-brain-does-not-process-information-and-it-is-not-a-computer. Accessed August 2016.

Esterson. A. (1998) Jeffrey Masson and Freud's Seduction Theory: A new fable based on old myths. *History of the Human Sciences*, 11(1), pp.1-21.

Express Tribune (2012) Church hounding of Pussy Riot troubles Russians. 14 August. http://tribune.com.pk/story/422105/church-hounding-of-pussy-riot-troubles-russians/. Accessed January 2015.

Felsenthal, J. (2015) Laurie Anderson Takes On Love and Death in *Heart of a Dog*. *Vogue*. http://www.vogue.com/13362723/laurie-anderson-heart-of-a-dog/. Accessed June 2016.

Ferguson, C. (2016) Our Struggle between Science and Pseudoscience. *The Psychologist*, 29(5), pp.362-5.

Fischer, E. (2010) *The Necessity of Art*. London. Verso.

Foucault, M. (2002) *The Archaeology of Knowledge*. London. Routledge.

Fransella, F. (1973) *Need to Change*. London. Methuen.

Freud, S. (1896) The Aetiology of Hysteria. Reprinted in: J. Masson (1992) *The Assault on Truth*. London. Fontana.

—. (1975) *The Psychopathology of Everyday Life*. Harmondsworth. Penguin.

—. (1983) *The Interpretation of Dreams*. Harmondsworth. Penguin.

—. (1990) *Five Lectures on Psychoanalysis*. New York. W. W. Norton.

—. (2003) *The Uncanny*. London. Penguin.

—. (2012) *A General Introduction to Psychoanalysis*. Ware. Wordsworth.

Freud, S. & Breuer, J. (2004) *Studies in Hysteria*. London. Penguin.

Fromm, E. (1973) *The Crisis of Psychoanalysis*. Harmondsworth. Penguin.

—. (1995) *The Art of Loving*. London. Harper Collins.

—. (2004) *The Fear of Freedom*. London. Routledge.

—. (2013) *To Have or To Be?* London. Bloomsbury.

Galeano, E. (1992) *The Book of Embraces*. New York and London. W.W. Norton & Co Ltd.

Gergen, K.J. (1973) Social Psychology as History. *Journal of Personality and Social Psychology*, 26(2), pp.309-20.

Gibson, J.J. (2015) *The Ecological Approach to Visual Perception*. Classic edition. London. Psychology Press.

Giroux, H. A. (2014) *Neoliberalism's War on Higher Education*. Chicago. Haymarket Books.

Gjesdal, K. (2014) Hermeneutics, Individuality and Tradition: Schleiermacher's Idea of Bildung in the landscape of Hegelian thought. In: D. Nassar (ed.) *The Relevance of Romanticism:*

Essays on German Romantic philosophy. Oxford. Oxford University Press.

Glaser, E. (2015) Bureaucracy: Why won't scholars break their paper chains? *Times Higher Education.* 21 May. https://www.timeshighereducation.com/features/bureaucracy-why-wont-scholars-break-their-paper-chains/2020256.article. Accessed May 2016.

Glendinning, S. (2011) *Derrida: A very short introduction.* Oxford. Oxford University Press.

Goldhagen, D.J. (1996) *Hitler's Willing Executioners.* London. Abacus.

Griffin, J. (1997) *The Origin of Dreams.* Worthing. The Therapist Ltd.

Guéry, F. & Deleule, D. (2014) *The Productive Body.* Winchester. Zero Books.

Guilfoyle, A. (1979) *Peaceable Kingdom.* London. Macmillan.

Gutting, G. (2005) *Foucault: A very short introduction.* Oxford. Oxford University Press.

Harper, D., Roberts, R. & Sloboda, J. (2007) A Psychology for Peace. In: R. Roberts (ed.) *Just War: Psychology and terrorism.* Ross-On-Wye. PCCS Books.

Haughton, H. (2003) Introduction. In: S. Freud. *The Uncanny.* London. Penguin.

Hayes, G. (2003) Walking the Streets: Psychology and the flâneur. *Annual Review of Critical Psychology,* 3, pp.50-66.

Heath, M. (1996) Introduction. In: Aristotle. *Poetics.* London. Penguin.

Hell, J. & Schönle, A. (eds.) (2010) *Ruins of Modernity.* Durham and London. Duke University Press.

Henri, H. (1967) Where'er You Walk. In: A. Henri, R. McGough & B. Patten. *Penguin Modern Poets 10: The Mersey Sound.* Harmondsworth. Penguin.

Hepburn, A. (2003) *An Introduction to Critical Social Psychology.* London. Sage.

Hewstone, M., Stroebe, W. & Stephenson, G.M. (1996) *Introduction to Social Psychology* (2nd ed.). Oxford. Blackwell Publishers.

Hillman, J. & Shamdasani, S. (2013) *Lament of the Dead: Psychology after Jung's* Red Book. New York and London. W.W. Norton & Co Ltd.

Hobart, P. (2003) *Kishido: The way of the Western warrior*. Prescott. Hohm Press.

Hofstadter, D. (1981) *Gödel, Escher, Bach: An eternal golden braid*. London. Penguin.

Hogg, M.A. & Vaughan, G.M. (2010) *Essentials of Social Psychology*. Harlow. Pearson Education Ltd.

Holquist, M. & Kliger, I. (2005) Minding the Gap: Toward a historical poetics of estrangement. *Poetics Today*, 26(4), pp.613-36.

Horwitz, A.C. & Wakefield, J.C. (2007) *The Loss of Sadness: How psychiatry transformed normal sorrow into depressive disorder*. Oxford. Oxford University Press.

Hutton, W. (2015) *How Good We Can Be: Ending the mercenary society and building a great country*. London. Little, Brown.

Hyams, J. (1982) *Zen in the Martial Arts*. London. Bantam Books.

Itten, T. & Roberts, R. (2014) *The New Politics of Experience & the Bitter Herbs*. Monmouth. PCCS Books.

Jackins, H. (1997) *The List*. Seattle. Rational Island Publishers.

James, O. (2014) Guest Blog. *Psychology Cultures.* University of Leicester. https://psychologycultures.wordpress.com/2014/03/19/guest-blog-by-oliver-james/. Accessed May 2015.

Janov, A. (2003) *The New Primal Scream*. London. Abacus.

Jones, O. (2005) An Ecology of Emotion, Memory, Self and Landscape. In: L. Bondi, J. Davidson & M. Smith (eds.) *Emotional Geographies*. Farnham. Ashgate.

Jung, C.G. (1995) *Memories, Dreams, Reflections*. London. Fontana Press.

Jwing-Ming, Y. (1982) *Shaolin Chin Na: The seizing art of kung-fu*.

Burbank. Unique Publications.

Kaufmann, K. & New, C. (2004) *Co-Counselling*. Hove and New York. Brunner-Routledge.

Kelly, G.A. (1955) *The Psychology of Personal Constructs*. New York. W.W. Norton & Co.

—. (1977) The Psychology of the Unknown. In: D. Bannister (ed.) *New Perspectives in Personal Construct Theory*. London. Academic Press.

Kirsner, D. (2015) Laing's *The Divided Self* and *The Politics of Experience*: Then and now. In: M. Guy Thompson (ed.) *The Legacy of R.D. Laing*. London. Routledge.

Kit W.K. (1981) *Introduction to Shaolin Kung Fu*. Dorset. Caric Press.

—. (2001) *The Art of Shaolin Kung Fu*. London. Random House.

Kleon, A. (2012) *Steal Like an Artist*. New York. Workman Publishing Company.

Konzak , B. & Boudreau, F. (1984) Martial Arts Training and Mental Health: An exercise in self-help. *Canada's Mental Health*, 32, pp.2-8.

Kornfield, J. (2008) *The Wise Heart*. Rider Books. London.

Kotsko, A. (2015) *Creepiness*. Winchester. Zero Books.

Kozma, A. (2013) *Warrior Guards the Mountain*. London and Philadelphia. Singing Dragon.

Kundera, M. (1996) *The Book of Laughter and Forgetting*. London. Faber and Faber.

Laing, R.D. (1965) Mystification, Confusion and Conflict. In: I. Boszormenyinagi & J.L. Framo (eds.). *Intensive Family Therapy: Theoretical and practical aspects*. New York. Harper and Row.

—. (1971) *The Politics of the Family and Other Essays*. London. Tavistock.

—. (1971b) *Knots*. Harmondsworth. Penguin.

Laing, R. D. & Esterson, A. (1964) *Sanity, Madness and the Family*. London. Tavistock.

Lampinen, P. (2002) What Exactly Is *Déjà Vu*? *Scientific American*.

13 May. http://www.scientificamerican.com/article/what-exactly-is-dj-vu/. Accessed May 2015.

Lee, B. (1997) *The Tao of Gung Fu*. Boston. Tuttle Publishing.

Macarie, J-C, and Roberts, R. (2010) Martial Arts and Mental Health. *Contemporary Psychotherapy*, 2, p.1. http://contemporarypsychotherapy.org/vol-2-no-1/martial-arts-and-mental-health/.

Mandelstam, O. (1991) *Selected Poems*. London. Penguin.

Mason, P. (2015) *Postcapitalism: A guide to our future*. London. Allen Lane.

Masson, J. (1992) *The Assault on Truth*. London. Fontana.

Mesquita, G.R. (2012) Vygotsky and the Theories of Emotions: In search of a possible dialogue. *Psicologia: Reflexão e Critica*, 25(4). http://www.scielo.br/scielo.php?script=sci_arttext&pid=S0102-79722012000400021. Accessed July 2016.

Middleton D. & Brown, S.D. (2005) *The Social Psychology of Experience: Studies in remembering and forgetting*. London. Sage.

Miller, D. (2000) *The Tao of Bruce Lee*. Vintage. London.

—. (2009) *The Comfort of Things*. Cambridge. Polity Press.

Mitchell, J. (2000) *Psychoanalysis and Feminism*. New York. Basic Books.

Moscovici, S. & Duveen, G. (eds.) (2000) *Social Representations: Explorations in social psychology*. Cambridge. Polity.

Mullan, B. (1995) *Mad to Be Normal: Conversations with R.D. Laing*. London. Free Association.

Mullarkey, J. (1999) *The New Bergson*. Manchester and New York. Manchester University Press.

Nietzsche, F. (1968) *Twilight of the Idols and the Anti-Christ*. Harmondsworth. Penguin.

Ornstein. R. (1972) *The Psychology of Consciousness*. San Francisco. W.H. Freeman.

Pao, J. (2010) *The Tao of Kung Fu*. London. Self-published.

Parker, I. (2007) *Revolution in Psychology: Alienation to emancipation*. London: Pluto Press.

Paterson, M. (2005) Affecting Touch: Towards a "felt" phenomenology of therapeutic touch. In: L. Bondi, J. Davidson & M. Smith (eds.). *Emotional Geographies*. Farnham. Ashgate.

Patten, B. (1981) *Vanishing Trick*. London. Unwin Paperbacks.

—. (2007) *Collected Love Poems*. London. Harper Perennial.

Payne, P. (1997) *Martial Arts: The spiritual dimension*. London. Thames and Hudson Ltd.

Polyani, M. (1962) *Personal Knowledge: Toward a post-critical philosophy*. London. Routledge.

Porter, R. (1996) The Assault on Jeffrey Masson. In: N.R. Keddie (ed.). *Debating Gender, Debating Sexuality*. New York and London. New York University Press. pp.277-95.

Potter, B. (2015) *Elements of Reparation*. London. Karnac.

Rabinow, P. (ed.) (1991) *The Foucault Reader*. London. Penguin.

Reich, W. (1974) *Listen, Little Man*. New York. Farrar, Straus and Giroux.

—. (1975) *The Mass Psychology of Fascism*. Harmondsworth. Penguin.

Roberts, R. (2015) *Psychology and Capitalism*. Winchester. Zero Books.

Roberts, R. & Hewer, H. (2015) Memory, "Madness" and Conflict: A Laingian perspective. *Memory Studies*, 8(2), pp.169-82.

Roberts, R. & Itten, T. (2006) Laing and Szasz: Anti-Psychiatry, capitalism and therapy. *The Psychoanalytic Review*, 93(5), pp.781-99.

Russell, G.W. (1993) *The Social Psychology of Sport*. New York. Springer-Verlag.

Ruttenburg, N. (2005) Dostoevsky's Estrangement. *Poetics Today*, 26(4) pp.719-52.

Safran, J.D. & Greenberg, L.S. (1991) Affective Change Processes: A synthesis and critical analysis. In: J.D. Safran & L.S. Greenberg (eds.). *Emotion, Psychotherapy and Change*. New York and London. The Guildford Press.

Scheff, T.J. (2001) *Catharsis in Healing, Ritual, and Drama*. Lincoln.

Authors Guild.

Schopenhauer, A. (1995) *Essays on Freedom of the Will*. London. John Wiley.

Shan, K.K. (2002) *The Cat and the Tao*. London. William Heinemann.

Sharaf, M. (1994) *Fury on Earth: A biography of Wilhelm Reich*. Cambridge. Da Capo Press.

Sheldrake, R. (2012) *The Science Delusion*. London. Coronet.

Shklovsky, V. (2005) *Knight's Move*. London. Dalkey Archive Press.

—. (2015) *Theory of Prose*. London. Dalkey Archive Press.

Slingerland, E. (2003) *Effortless Action: Wu-Wei as conceptual metaphor and spiritual ideal in early China*. Oxford. Oxford University Press.

—. (2014) *Trying Not to Try: The ancient art of effortlessness and the surprising power of spontaneity*. Edinburgh. Canongate Books.

—. (2015) Wu-Wei: Doing less and wanting more. *The Psychologist*, 28(11), pp.882-5.

Smail, D. (2005) *Power Interest and Psychology*. Ross-on-Wye. PCCS Books.

Smith, S. (1978) *Selected Poems*. London. Penguin.

Solnit, R. (2006) *A Field Guide to Getting Lost*. Edinburgh and London. Canongate.

—. (2013) *The Faraway Nearby*. London. Granta.

—. (2014) *Wanderlust*. London. Granta.

—. (2016) *Hope in the Dark: Untold histories, wild possibilities*. London. Canongate.

Sophocles (2008) *Antigone, Oedipus the King and Electra*. Oxford. Oxford University Press.

Spinney, L. (2015) Once Upon a Time. *New Scientist*, 225(3003), pp.28-31.

Starosta, A. (2007) Gardens of Things: The vicissitudes of disappearance. *Intermédialités : histoire et théorie des arts, des lettres et des techniques / Intermediality: History and Theory of the Arts, Literature and Technologies*, 10, pp.147-63.

Staufenberg, J. (2016) Widespread media coverage contributing to rise in mass shootings, say psychologists. *The Independent*. http://www.independent.co.uk/news/science/mass-shooting-media-contagion-psychologists-research-personality-traits-us-a7172036.html.

Stratton, P. (2015) How broader research perspectives can free clients and psychotherapists to optimise their work together. In: T. Warnecke (ed.). *Psychotherapy and Society*. London. Karnac.

Sue, D. & Sue, S. (2016) *Understanding Abnormal Behaviour* (11th ed.). Stamford. Cengage.

Szasz, T. (2007) *The Medicalization of Everyday Life*. New York. Syracuse University Press.

—. (2009) *Anti-Psychiatry: Quackery squared*. New York. Syracuse University Press.

—. (2010) *The Myth of Mental Illness*. New York. Harper Perennial.

Thomas, D. (2000) *Collected Poems 1934-1953*. London. Phoenix.

—. (2003) *The Poems of Dylan Thomas*. New York. New Directions.

Tucker, (2012) Bully U. Central Planning and Higher Education. *The Independent Review*, 17(1), pp.99-119.

Unger, R.M. & Smolin, L. (2015) *The Singular Universe and the Reality of Time*. Cambridge University Press. Cambridge.

Urry, J. (2005) The Place of Emotions within Place. In: L. Bondi, J. Davidson & M. Smith (eds.). *Emotional Geographies*. Farnham. Ashgate.

Vatulescu, C. (2005) The Politics of Estrangement: Tracking Shklovsky's device through literary and policing practices. *Poetics Today*, 27(1), pp.35-66.

Vitz, P. C. (1994) *Psychology as Religion: The cult of self-worship* (2nd ed.). Grand Rapids, MI. William B. Eerdmans Publishing and

The Paternoster Press.

Reps, P. (1971) *Zen Flesh Zen Bones*. London. Penguin.

Whitehead, A.N. (1968) *Modes of Thought*. Toronto. Collier-MacMillan.

Wile, D. (2007) Tajiquan and Daoism. *Journal of Asian Martial Arts*, 16(4), pp.8-45.

Winnicott, D. (1953) Transitional Objects and Transitional Phenomena: A study of the first not-me possession. *International Journal of Psychoanalysis*, 34(2), pp.89-97.

—. (1986) *Home Is Where We Start From*. Harmondsworth. Penguin.

Winokur, G. & Clayton, P. (1994) *The Medical Basis of Psychiatry* (2nd ed.). Philadelphia. WB Saunders.

Winters, J.A. (2011) *Oligarchy*. New York. Cambridge University Press.

Woolf, V. (2013) *To the Lighthouse*. London. Harper Press.

Zeldin, T. (1995) *An Intimate History of Humanity*. London. Vintage.

Žižek, S. (2010) *Living in the End Times*. London. Verso.

Zukav, G. (1984) *The Dancing Wu Li Masters*. London. Flamingo.

Zero Books
CULTURE, SOCIETY & POLITICS
Contemporary culture has eliminated the concept and public figure of
the intellectual. A cretinous anti-intellectualism presides, cheer-led by
hacks in the pay of multinational corporations who reassure their
bored readers that there is no need to rouse themselves from their
stupor. Zer0 Books knows that another kind of discourse - intellectual
without being academic, popular without being populist - is not only
possible: it is already flourishing. Zer0 is convinced that in the
unthinking, blandly consensual culture in which we live, critical and
engaged theoretical reflection is more important than ever before.
If you have enjoyed this book, why not tell other readers by
posting a review on your preferred book site. Recent bestsellers from
Zero Books are:

In the Dust of This Planet
Horror of Philosophy vol. 1
Eugene Thacker
In the first of a series of three books on the Horror of
Philosophy, *In the Dust of This Planet* offers the genre of horror
as a way of thinking about the unthinkable.
Paperback: 978-1-84694-676-9 ebook: 978-1-78099-010-1

Capitalist Realism
Is there no alternative?
Mark Fisher
An analysis of the ways in which capitalism has presented itself
as the only realistic political-economic system.
Paperback: 978-1-84694-317-1 ebook: 978-1-78099-734-6

Rebel Rebel
Chris O'Leary
David Bowie: every single song. Everything you want to know, everything you didn't know.
Paperback: 978-1-78099-244-0 ebook: 978-1-78099-713-1

Cartographies of the Absolute
Alberto Toscano, Jeff Kinkle
An aesthetics of the economy for the twenty-first century.
Paperback: 978-1-78099-275-4 ebook: 978-1-78279-973-3

Malign Velocities
Accelerationism and Capitalism
Benjamin Noys
Long listed for the Bread and Roses Prize 2015, *Malign Velocities* argues against the need for speed, tracking acceleration as the symptom of the on-going crises of capitalism.
Paperback: 978-1-78279-300-7 ebook: 978-1-78279-299-4

Meat Market
Female flesh under Capitalism
Laurie Penny
A feminist dissection of women's bodies as the fleshy fulcrum of capitalist cannibalism, whereby women are both consumers and consumed.
Paperback: 978-1-84694-521-2 ebook: 978-1-84694-782-7

Poor but Sexy
Culture Clashes in Europe East and West
Agata Pyzik
How the East stayed East and the West stayed West.
Paperback: 978-1-78099-394-2 ebook: 978-1-78099-395-9

Romeo and Juliet in Palestine
Teaching Under Occupation
Tom Sperlinger
Life in the West Bank, the nature of pedagogy and the role of a
university under occupation.
Paperback: 978-1-78279-637-4 ebook: 978-1-78279-636-7

Sweetening the Pill
or How we Got Hooked on Hormonal Birth Control
Holly Grigg-Spall
Has contraception liberated or oppressed women? *Sweetening
the Pill* breaks the silence on the dark side of hormonal
contraception.
Paperback: 978-1-78099-607-3 ebook: 978-1-78099-608-0

Why Are We The Good Guys?
Reclaiming your Mind from the Delusions of Propaganda
David Cromwell
A provocative challenge to the standard ideology that Western
power is a benevolent force in the world.
Paperback: 978-1-78099-365-2 ebook: 978-1-78099-366-9

Readers of ebooks can buy or view any of these bestsellers by
clicking on the live link in the title. Most titles are published in
paperback and as an ebook. Paperbacks are available in traditional
bookshops. Both print and ebook formats are available online.

Find more titles and sign up to our readers' newsletter at
http://www.johnhuntpublishing.com/culture-and-politics
Follow us on Facebook at https://www.facebook.com/ZeroBooks
and Twitter at https://twitter.com/Zer0Books